17163

THE
FUND
FOR
ADULT EDUCATION

A Study of Participants in the Great Books Program

1957

By

National Opinion Research Center

JAMES A. DAVIS
Senior Study Director

with the assistance of LATHROP VICKERY BEALE
RUTH URSULA GEBHARD

Library of Congress Catalog Card No. 60-16560

Copyright ©1960
The Fund for Adult Education

Preface

BY

C. SCOTT FLETCHER
PRESIDENT
THE FUND FOR
ADULT EDUCATION

This book represents one of four "Studies in Adult Group Learning in the Liberal Arts" being published in 1960 by The Fund for Adult Education. The first one was an analytical history of the study-discussion programs developed by the Fund's Experimental Discussion Project: *Accent on Learning,* by the Director of the Project, Dr. Glen Burch. The other three are research studies, resulting from independent investigations conducted by highly competent research groups in the social sciences. Together they represent the first serious attempt to apply the methods of social science research to the evaluation of adult education programs: in this case, programs of reading and discussion in small groups led by non-professional students of the subject matter rather than by experts in it.

Established in 1951 by The Ford Foundation, the Fund was assigned a concern with "that part of the educational process which begins when formal schooling is finished." The Fund's Board of Directors defined their purpose as that of "supporting programs of liberal adult education which will contribute to the development of mature, wise, and responsible citizens who can participate intelligently in a free society." To these ends, the Fund has laid particular emphasis upon study-discussion programs in the liberal arts. It has done so not only through its own Project, but also by giving substantial financial assistance to universities, liberal arts centers, and national organizations which sponsored and promoted such programs, developed program materials, and trained leaders.

In 1959-60, the Great Books Foundation enrolled 50,000 participants in 2,700 groups in more than a thousand communities, in the United States and abroad. The American Foundation for Continuing Education had more than 10,000 group participants in nearly five hundred communities. Universities, colleges, public libraries, public evening schools, and a host of local social and civic agencies and educational groups, including private persons and their friends, have organized and sponsored the group study of these materials. In 1959, more than 15,000 men and women were engaged in the study and discussion programs brought into being by the Fund. While these were, for an experimental period, confined to ten "Test Centers" (mentioned in Burch's study, and described more fully in the Fund's biennial Report for 1955-57 and in a document to be issued later this year), by 1958 a rapidly growing list of other educational organizations, national and local, and of private groups, were using these programs. At the present time, twelve of the programs are being published or prepared for publication by commercial publishers; and the audio-visual components of the programs are being distributed by the Audio-Visual Center at the University of Indiana.

With the spread of study-discussion programs in the liberal arts came recognition of the need for careful study of the values and the effects of this method for the people who took part. As more colleges and universities moved to set up programs of this type, concern was felt by many faculty members over the maintenance of high educational standards, particularly where the group leadership was in the hands of those who were not professional educators. The Fund, therefore, as early as 1955, began a series of research grants for studies of the participants, the leaders, and the educational effectiveness of study-discussion programs, the studies being made by independent investigators not themselves connected with the program. Three major studies were made between 1955 and 1959.

The first study, made in 1956 by members of the faculties of the University of California at Los Angeles, the California Institute of Technology, and Whittier College, was directed by Abbott Kaplan, then Assistant Director of Extension at UCLA. The field of the studies consisted of 118 liberal arts groups, in four content areas: *World Affairs, World*

Politics, Ways of Mankind, and *Introduction to the Humanities.* The specific sample included 150 individuals who were members of groups in Los Angeles, Pasadena, and Whittier, and fifty of the group leaders: the method was based on 325 interviews, before, during, and after the ten-week program, and observation of 52 group sessions.

The second study was made in 1957 by the National Opinion Research Center of Chicago, using some 1900 participants in 172 *Great Books* groups, ranging from first-year to fifth-year status within that program. Interviewers visited the groups and administered detailed questionnaires; and the responses were coded on IBM cards and subjected to elaborate statistical analysis. The director of this study was Dr. James A. Davis.

The third major study, in 1958, was designed to compare learning effects of the same content, *Ways of Mankind,* with two methods: university lecture and lay-led group discussion. The sample studied consisted of three lecture classes, enrolling 283 adults, and twelve discussion groups with 293 participants, all within the liberal arts program of UCLA. Again, use was made of questionnaires, interviews, and direct observation. The director of this study was Dr. Richard J. Hill,* Department of Anthropology and Sociology, UCLA.

The publication of these studies, which were separately conceived and independently carried out, is not intended as a plea for one method over others. It is intended as a contribution to the discussion, among educators and interested adult students, of the appropriate place and use and purpose of one of the many methods of learning that appeal to men and women, and as an aid to educators and administrators in their choices of program methods and student "publics". Here, for the first time, are presented — though in admittedly preliminary form — responsible research data and statistical interpretation on adults in liberal arts programs. The studies themselves make it clear that the reading-discussion method attracts a particular kind of audience, and that the larger population from which it is drawn has many other tastes and proclivities. The question, therefore, is not, "Which method is best?" but, "What is the best type of program and method for given sorts of people, and what ends are best served by which educational means?"

If this broader question were studied for many types of education and many kinds of educational publics, our skill and effectiveness in adult education would be immeasurably advanced. It is to this greatly needed research effort that we hope to contribute by offering these studies to the public.

---

*Dr. Hill is now with the Department of Sociology, University of Texas.

Acknowledgments

The "credits" for any national survey bulk as large as those of an MGM musical. We should like, however, to note the special contributions of the following:

G. H. Griffiths, Vice-president of The Fund for Adult Education, and Professor Carl Hovland of Yale University, research consultant to the Fund, were constant aids throughout the study. At one time or another, most of the staff of the Great Books Foundation was involved in our survey, but we should like to thank Dr. James Jarrett, Mr. Orace Johnson, Mrs. Freda Goldman, and Miss Lily Durr for their special assistance. In addition, Mr. Leonard Stein of the University of Chicago Home Study Center, Professor James Coleman of the University of Chicago, Professor Peter H. Rossi of the University of Chicago, Mr. Charles E. Martin of New York City, and Professor M. R. Trabue helped us in many ways.

The entire staff of the National Opinion Research Center contributed in one way or another to the study, but special debts of gratitude are owed to: Mrs. Mary Booth, who supervised the sampling and initial coding; Mrs. Grace Lieberman, who supervised the field work; Irene Skolnick, Carolyn Goetz, Sarah Field, Mrs. Ada Farber, Jonathan Wallach, and Sultan Hashmi, our merry and meticulous coding crew; Harold Levy, Sanford Abrams, and Fred Meier, of NORC's machine-room staff; Morris Sunshine, graduate student of Northwestern University; Joseph Zelan, our indefatigable research assistant; Mrs. Georgia Grann, tireless proofreader; Mrs. Ada B. Caplow and Mrs. Nella V. Siefert, probably the best typists around; and Carolyn Huson, who aided in the calculations of the follow-up data. Although not members of the project staff, Clyde W. Hart, Director, and Jacob J. Feldman, Senior Study Director, at NORC, were continual and vital consultants.

Since this is an evaluation study, with some potential implications for policy decisions in the world of adult education, the following responsibilities should be specifically acknowledged: The entire report is the sole responsibility of the National Opinion Research Center, and specifically that of the study director. Staff members of The Fund for Adult Education and the Great Books Foundation aided us considerably but did not review or edit the report, aside from technical editing for publication of this summary. Ruth Ursula Gebhard did the preliminary analysis of the data on poetry, and Lathrop V. Beale did the first drafts of the analysis of reading and community involvement. The remainder of the report was analyzed and written by the study director. Blame should be addressed to the proper person, but since the three of us consulted together day in and day out, any credit should go jointly to the three authors.

James A. Davis
February, 1959

Contents

*In childhood and youth their study, and what philosophy
they learn, should be suited to their tender years: during
this period while they are growing up towards manhood, the
chief and special care should be given to their bodies that they
may have them to use in the service of philosophy; as life
advances and the intellect begins to mature, let them increase
the gymnastics of the soul.*

The Republic
Book VI

Introduction

INTRODUCTION

Background

In the summer of 1957, The Fund for Adult Education, an independent educational foundation established by The Ford Foundation, commissioned the National Opinion Research Center of the University of Chicago to make a study of the Great Books program. The major purpose of the study was to assess the effects of participation in the program in order to provide information to guide future policy in the field of adult education. The study specifically excludes any consideration of the administration or functioning of the Great Books Foundation, which sponsors the program, but rather is concentrated on the participants and their discussion groups.

A report on the survey was completed in September, 1958. Subsequently The Fund for Adult Education commissioned a follow-up study of the groups interviewed in 1957. Since a final report, including the follow-up study, would not be ready until late 1959, it was decided to make available a condensed version of the 1958 report. The condensation was effected by omitting a good many of the statistical tables and detailed descriptions of some of the analytical procedures used. But it is hoped that, for the general reader, the positive findings and the evidence on which they are based are adequately covered. Readers who are interested in the detailed analyses in the original report should consult The Fund for Adult Education.

The Great Books program itself is so well known that it need not be described in detail. Great Books, which was originally developed by Mortimer Adler and Robert M. Hutchins, then of the University of Chicago, is a national program for the liberal education of adults. In 1957-58 it consisted of some 1,960 discussion groups dispersed through the United States, with additional groups in Canada and overseas. Each group meets every other week from September to June, and at each meeting the members discuss a specific selection which they have read before the meeting. These readings are organized into blocks of one year each and, in theory, should be read in sequence. Since members often enter on-going groups, however, the correlation between specific readings and years in the program is less than perfect. In our study we have focused on total number of years completed rather than on the specific readings.[1]

The groups vary in size (from around five to around thirty-five, with an average of about eleven in our sample); in sponsorship (most are affiliated with public libraries, but a number are sponsored by churches, business firms, and individuals); and in leadership (some have a single leader, most have co-leaders, and a few rotate the leadership with each meeting); but generally they follow the pattern of small, informal discussion groups.

In order to understand the nature of the program, we should stress the following characteristics: The leaders are not formally trained teachers, but a number have had brief training courses sponsored by the Great Books Foundation, and many are long-time participants who are now leading groups studying earlier years of the readings. The members do not pay any tuition or get any degree or certificate for completing the program. In fact, no one can "complete" the program, as additional years of reading are always available, currently up to the fourteenth year. Members are encouraged to buy the readings from the Foundation but are not required to do so. The Great Books Foundation itself is a non-profit organization, which attempts to stimulate the formation of groups, and provides readings and publicity materials. It also provides advice and help to groups from the national office or through local community coordinators in larger cities. Some coordinators are full-time members of the Foundation staff, some are volunteers or have other jobs in adult education.

---

[1] The curriculum of reading as of 1957-58 is reproduced as Appendix 1 of this report.

Procedures

During December, 1957, NORC interviewers attended the meetings of 172 groups, sampled in a manner described below. Members had not been informed before the meeting that they were to participate in the research on that night, although some knew their group would be called on at some time. Each member of the sampled groups filled out the self-administered questionnaire which is reproduced as Appendix 2 to this report. By and large, cooperation was found to be good. Although a number of groups were visibly disappointed that they had to forego their discussion, only one protocol was rejected because inspection indicated that the writer did not give serious cooperation. One other schedule, from a member whose physical handicap resulted in an illegible questionnaire, was excluded, leaving a total of 1,909 cases from 172 groups.

The questionnaires were coded and punched onto IBM cards for analysis. The materials presented here are based on statistical analyses of these cards. Coding, punching, and card-cleaning were completed by June, 1958, and analysis and write-up took place during June, July, and early August, 1958.

Sample

NORC is set up to take probability samples of the general population of the United States. In order to do so, it maintains a permanent field staff of trained interviewers in a national sample of counties and standard metropolitan areas. These are known as "primary sampling units." The counties were selected in such a way that by weighting the interviews, national estimates for a cross-section of the general population are efficiently and accurately obtained, subject, of course, to random sampling error.

Our sample is a probability sample (stratified by year of reading) of the Great Books discussion groups which, in November and December, 1957, were meeting in the metropolitan areas and counties outside of metropolitan areas that comprise NORC's "primary sampling units." Since each member of the sampled groups was asked to fill out a schedule, the number of individuals each group contributed to the total sample was obviously proportional to its size, hence our sample is also representative of "individuals" as well as groups, although this procedure results in the sample of individuals being heavily clustered.

For technical reasons which are inherent in any such sample drawn by any research agency, bias is introduced when one attempts to sample a universe with a relatively small population of individuals, such as Great Books groups. The net effect of this bias is that, while the cases sampled are representative of cases in their type of county in the country, too many cases are drawn from large cities and too few cases are drawn from small towns and rural areas. In judging the seriousness of this bias, the following considerations should be kept in mind:

1. The Great Books program itself is disproportionately urban. Thus, in 1955, the last year for which NORC had available complete data on the program, the standard metropolitan areas of the United States, which included 56 per cent of the U.S. 1950 population, had 75 per cent of the Great Books groups.

2. Our budget precluded the use of trained interviewers for a true national sample, and we felt that it was preferable to have national coverage, even with an urban bias, rather than to have perfect sampling of a limited geographical area, such as the Midwest.

While sampling bias is hardly desirable, from a practical point of view it is only when the bias affects important characteristics of the population that it becomes a serious problem. Thus, if our sample contained a disproportionate number of left-handed people but was representative in every other way, the bias would be unimportant, since handedness is not a concern of our research.

In order to estimate the practical bias in our sample, we compared selected characteristics of respondents in cities of different size. We found no consistent differences in the following: (1) age, (2) education, (3) feeling that the program has had a high impact, (4) scores on the test of knowledge of the liberal arts and humanities, (5) self-definition as "intellectual" or "non-intellectual," and (6) interest in community affairs.

We did find the following differences: (1) Jews are less frequent in the smaller towns than in the large urban areas; (2) Republicans are more frequent in smaller towns; and (3) married participants are more frequent in smaller towns. Our data thus tend to over-estimate the proportion of Jews, Democrats, and non-married in the program. Where these differences might affect the conclusions, the type of city is considered in detail in the analysis.

In the fall of 1957, we listed all of the groups in NORC sample points which were registered with the Great Books Foundation. One hundred eighty-two groups were selected by a probability process which deliberately over-represented advanced-year groups, with the aim of netting fifty first-year groups, thirty each in years II through IV, and thirty in years V and more. Sixteen of the groups were not interviewed for the following reasons: five were defunct, one was found to be a duplicate registration of another group in the sample, one was not a Great Books group, two had participated in the pre-test for the study, six were unable to schedule a date for the field work (three of them did not meet during the field period), and one leader refused. Seven of these groups were replaced, and one of our sample groups had split in two, both parts being interviewed. This gave us a total of 172 groups.

Analysis

This summary treats three parts of the original report. Part A ("The Participants") describes the social characteristics of the people in the program and compares them with other members of the American population. Part B ("Self-Assessments") examines the respondents' reports on their motives for joining and their own reports on the effects of participation. Part C ("Statistical Assessments") attempts to arrive at indirect measures of the effects of program participation.

Stated in somewhat more specific terms, this summary is organized around the basic questions which guided the study:

What are the Participants Like?

Throughout the study we have stressed the "social characteristics" of the members, their stage in the life cycle, their memberships, their institutional affiliations, and their self-conceptions. This is because we feel it is not only important to know what the effects are, but also what sorts of people are being affected. In particular, we have continually stressed "institutional" characteristics, or the ways in which the members are related to the major organizations of their community and society . . . their churches, their jobs, their political parties, and their community activities. This is because we believe that a liberal education is not only to be consumed but also to be acted on, and it is important to know in what areas of the larger community and society we may expect to find Great Books participants. The problem of the relationships between "books and action" has been a constant preoccupation of the study.

What are their Cultural Abilities and Interests?

At times we have thought of the participants not just as Great Books members but as specimens of highly educated Americans. We have absolutely no statistical grounds for presenting them collectively as a representative sample of the highly educated, but we did look among them for clues to answers to some general problems that go beyond the scope of the program itself. We live in a time when continual cries of rage and anger are heard claiming that Americans are deficient in their interests in what one can call "high culture." Now there is quite a lot in print about "highbrows," because highbrows tend to draw attention to themselves. There is also a lot in print about "lowbrows" because they are the happy hunting-ground of the sociologist. Not a lot, however, is known about the cultural life of the "middlebrow," the Book-of-the-Month reader, the occasional concert-goer, the subscriber to *Harper's* and *The Saturday Review*. Since, for all practical purposes, our group of Great Books participants consists of 1,909 such people, we have at times gone out of our way to present basic descriptive materials on their cultural characteristics and orientations, and the patternings thereof.

What are the Effects of Great Books on the Participants?

We have come at this problem in two ways. First, we have simply asked the participants what they think the effects are. These materials are re-ported in Part B. Second, we have contrasted beginning and advanced par-ticipants. We know that the only sure answers about effects must come from a study following the same persons through time. Such a study was, how-ever, impossible, and we have attempted to do what we could with "cross-sectional" data. In every case where statistical techniques would enable us to meet some of the difficulties arising from such a design, we have used them.

Some Technical Matters

This is a summary of a statistical report, and no amount of verbal jolli-fication in the text can conceal the fact that the report consists of explana-tions and comments about the tables, rather than the tables consisting of illustrations of matter which is developed in the text. Most of the tables that are retained consist of sets of percentages and do not require statistical training for interpretation. In a few places we have used advanced statistical techniques which could not be explained in complete detail. In these cir-cumstances we have attempted to present the general strategy in strictly verbal terms but have not explained the mathematics in full detail.

Unless the text indicates something to the contrary, in all tables the difference between the number of cases given in the table and 1,909 (the sample size) is due to those respondents who failed to answer the questions involved.

One final word before we begin our report. Although the study is de-signed to provide a better basis for evaluating the Great Books program, we have attempted to refrain, with the exception of one footnote, from doing any evaluating ourselves. Where we have found effects, we have attempted to present any findings which would tend to "minimize" them, and where we have not, we have attempted to present any findings which would tend to "mitigate" the blow. Any net assessment of the program must come from the reader.

Part A
THE
PARTICIPANTS

THE PARTICIPANTS

What are they like? What sorts of people are attracted to Great Books? In this chapter we shall attempt to describe the 1,909 participants in our sample in terms of their salient social characteristics . . . education, family situation, occupation, self conceptions, religious preference, and party preference. We have no data on their secret dreams and hidden motives, but we do have the basic bricks from which to build a sociological description of the members in terms of the roles which they play in their families, communities, and the larger society.

When we say "What are they like?" we usually mean "How are they different?", which, in turn, raises the question of "different from whom?" It is hardly necessary to document the ways in which 1,909 adult Americans differ from, say, 1,909 adult Chinese. What we would really like to know is how the people in Great Books differ from other people in their communities who had an opportunity to join, but did not. Thus, the question we raise really implies the necessity of having data from a control sample of people who might have been in the program, but were not. We have no such data in our study, but here and there we can contrast our materials with certain already published findings. The differences we find can be, at best, suggestive, given the methodological problems involved, but in this chapter we shall at least note them.

Education

Perhaps the most striking characteristic of the members is their high level of formal education. In the following table they are compared with 1950 Census data on the total U.S. population 25 years of age and over.

TABLE 1

Educational Attainment

Education	Number of Participants	Per cent of Participants	Per cent of U.S. Adult Population 1950
No college	297	16	86
Part college	433	24	7
Bachelor's degree	414	23⎱	
Graduate study	682	37⎰	6
	1,826	100%	99%
(No answer and uncodable)	83		
	1,909		

The contrast is plain. Eighty-four per cent of the participants have had at least some college, while 86 per cent of the total population have had none. Our sample even includes 100 Ph.D.s, who make up five per cent of the sample, while Ph.D.s account for roughly one-tenth of one per cent of the general population. Our data show no difference between the educational attainments of the beginning and advanced participants in Great Books discussion groups; hence, we may assume that while formal education has a lot to do with recruitment, it is not relevant *per se* for continuation.

This high education level is not shared equally by the sexes. As is generally true, men report higher educational attainments. More than half (54 per cent) of the men have had graduate work beyond the bachelor's degree, and 91 per cent have had some college training. Among the women, the percentages are lessened (27 per cent with graduate training, 79 per cent with some college).

Thus, it is perhaps fair to characterize Great Books as a program for, and almost limited to, "college people," the majority of whom have a bachelor's degree, and a considerable proportion of whom report graduate work or degrees beyond the bachelor's.

In order to assess the ways in which the participants view themselves subjectively, we asked them the following question:

Which of the following comes closest to the way you think about yourself?

1 — I don't like the phrase particularly, but I guess you'd have to call me an "intellectual."

2 — I consider myself an educated person, but not really an "intellectual."

3 — I haven't had too much education, so I can't really call myself either an "intellectual" or an "educated person," but I am pretty serious in my approach to things.

4 — I guess I'm sort of a "lowbrow" when it comes down to it.

We cannot assume that the respondents interpreted the terms of the question with real consistency, but they did at least choose their places in what they could easily recognize as a hierarchy of "intellectualness." In spite of their high educational levels, the bulk of the respondents (56 per cent) think of themselves as "educated people," and only a minority (15 per cent) consider themselves to be "intellectuals." The same general conclusion holds even when we take into consideration education and sex, two variables which relate to self-conception.

TABLE 2

Self-Conception by Sex and Education

Per cent considering themselves as "Intellectuals"

Education	Men	Women
No college	8 (61)	4 (219)
Part college	17 (101)	10 (309)
Bachelor's degree	13 (136)	8 (263)
Graduate work	28 (362)	19 (293)

(Base N in parentheses)

Throughout this report "N" refers to the base number on which the percentages were calculated.

On the whole, the proportion who think of themselves as intellectuals increases with education and is greater for men than for women within each educational level; however, even in the extreme group, men with graduate training, only slightly more than one-quarter claim to be "intellectuals."

Further confirmation of these interpretations comes from our data on "paths of life." We modified Charles Morris's value measurement scheme [1] and asked the respondents to rate four vignettes of values in terms of how much they liked or disliked them. The four can be labeled "Hedonism" ("Life is something to be enjoyed — sensuously enjoyed . . ."); "Groupy-

---

[1] The complete vignettes are reproduced in the schedule which is an appendix to this report. Cf., Charles Morris, *Varieties of Human Value*, Chicago: University of Chicago Press, 1956.

ness" ("A person should merge himself with a social group, enjoy cooperation and companionship . . ."); "Activity" ("A person must stress the need of constant activity — physical action, adventure, the realistic solution of specific problems . . ."); and "Contemplation" ("The contemplative life is the good life . . .").

TABLE 3

Marginal Distribution on "Paths of Life"

Per cent checking path . . .

Path	"Dislike it quite a lot" or "Dislike it very much"	"Dislike it slightly," "Indifferent," or "Like it slightly"	"Like it quite a lot" or "Like it very much"	N	Total per cent
"Groupyness"	8	45	46	1,813	99
"Activity"	14	50	36	1,799	100
"Hedonism"	30	45	25	1,792	100
"Contemplation"	30	51	19	1,785	100

Except for "groupyness," the participants are not wild about any of the values, but it does appear that the values associated with extremes of "intellectualism," either toward the "Bohemian" pole of hedonism or the "mystic" pole of contemplation, rank conspicuously low. Conversely, the modal American values of activity and group participation rank rather high, close to one-half of the participants endorsing "groupyness," and only eight per cent rejecting it. While we have no general American norms for this measure, our distinct impression is that the Great Books participants do not depart conspicuously from basic middle-class values, in which intellectual matters are certainly valued positively but do not form the core of the person's interests.

We have emphasized self-conception and values here, perhaps beyond their importance for the later analysis, but we would like to stress a point. Although there is some belief that the Great Books program attracts "ivory-tower" intellectuals and cult seekers, our evidence is essentially that the participants, although highly educated in comparison with the national population, share, on the whole, the general values and patterns of social participation of middle-class America.[2]

---

[2] If the point still needs clinching, we need only add that when asked about specific magazines, 69 per cent reported that they read the *Reader's Digest* regularly—or occasionally, and 65 per cent checked "Never heard of this one" for *The Partisan Review;* however, when we note that we have no national norms for "intellectualism," and we remember that the question was worded in such a way as to discourage checking answers at the "high" end, we cannot say whether there are more or fewer self-defined intellectuals in Great Books than in other populations. In fact, a recent article in the *American Journal of Sociology* can be read to imply that nearly as many participants who have had graduate training consider themselves to be intellectuals as assistant professors at Ohio State University. Cf., Melvin Seeman, "The Intellectual and the Language of Minorities," *American Journal of Sociology,* LXIV: 25-35, July, 1958.

Age, Sex, and Marital Status

Sociologists usually think of age, sex, and marital status as a cluster of variables which can be considered together as a person's "life cycle role." By this we mean only that, regardless of social status, region of residence, or religion, single, adolescent females have a lot in common, as do middle-aged, married males.

Sixty-three per cent of our sample are women, 37 per cent men, a disproportion which is undoubtedly "significant" in the sense that, although in the general population there are more women than men in the age ranges covered by Great Books, the disproportion is not so great as in the program. Or, to put it another way, more women than men join Great Books. When we compare beginning participants with advanced-year members, we find no important difference in the "sex ratio." Hence, our guess is that although more women are recruited initially, their drop-out rate is about the same as that of their masculine compatriots.[3]

Three-quarters (74 per cent) of the women are married, 15 per cent are single, and 11 per cent are widowed or divorced. The bulk of the married women are "housewives" with no part-time job or studies, while almost all of the single women are employed full-time, and most of the "ex-married" women are employed. Almost all the men work full time. There were very few "students" or "retired" in our sample. Of the men, 82 per cent are married, 14 per cent are single, and 5 per cent are widowed or divorced.

Table 4 is sort of a "collage" made up of sex, marital status, and occupation, in order to summarize the situation. We see that the bulk of the participants (65 per cent) consists of husbands and housewives, another 12 per cent of working wives, 13 per cent of "career" women, and the remaining 10 per cent of other categories. Putting it another way, we find 35 per cent housewives, 25 per cent working wives and career women, 30 per cent husbands, and 10 per cent others.

Before we leave the question of marital status, let us see how many of the married people participate as couples and how many do not. Table 5, below, summarizes these data.

For the married men, 54 per cent attend the group on a couple basis; for the married women, 36 per cent. The 264 "couples" thus make up 27 per cent of our entire sample. More married women attend without their husbands than married men without their wives. This discrepancy goes a long way toward explaining the sex ratio of the program. If each spouse in the sample attended with his or her mate, the increased number of males would change the proportion of women from the observed 63 per cent to

---

[3] Our analysis of the sample in the introduction suggests that there are relatively more men in the small towns, which are under-represented in our study. Even there, though, women form a slight majority.

TABLE 4

"Life Cycle Role" Distribution of the Participants

Type	Description	Per cent of Females	Per cent of Males	Per cent of Sample	N
1) Housewives	Married females reporting themselves as "housewives" with no job and not attending school	55	—	35	634
2) Working wives	Married females reporting full-time or part-time employment or full-time school attendance	19	—	12	214
3) Career women	Single women or ex-married women reporting full-time work	21	—	13	243
4) Other	Ex-married women reporting occupation as "housewife"	5	—	3	55
5) Husbands	Married males	—	82	30	556
6) Bachelors	Single males	—	14	5	93
7) Ex-married males	Males who are divorced or widowed	—	4	2	33
Insufficient information to classify					1,828 81
		100	100	100	1,909

54 per cent. Thus, our guess would be that the sex disproportion in the program is partly a function of the differential "joint attendance" of the two sexes.

TABLE 5

Husbands and Wives

	Spouse Member of Same Group and in Sample	Spouse Member of Same Group, but not in Sample*	Spouse Not a Member of the Group
Married males	264	35	257
Married females	264	37	547

* NORC interviewers collected from each leader the names of regular members of the group who were not present when the schedule was administered. By matching names, an estimate of "spouse loss" was made.

As one would expect from the above findings, the participants are concentrated in the early middle-age span. The age distribution, however, is somewhat biased, as our sample is deliberately inflated in the advanced years of participation. The longer-time participants are somewhat older than the beginners, although no more than one would expect from their years of exposure. (That is, there is no evidence in our data that younger people are more likely to drop out. The age difference in the "exposure" groups is a simple function of how long they have been in Great Books.)

A better perspective may be gained by comparing the first-year members with the "alumni" [4] in terms of their age distribution in the 1950 United States Census.

TABLE 6

Age Distribution of First-Year Great Books
Participants and U.S. College Alumni (1950)

Age	U.S.* college alumni	First-year participants**
25-34	34	42
35-44	28	30
45-54	19	16
55-64	11	7
65+	8	4
	100%	99% (N=675)

* *Statistical Abstract of the United States, 1950.*
** Forty-three participants under 25 were excluded to make the data comparable to the Census tables.

Great Books beginners, it appears, run a little younger than college alumni in general. Thus, both relatively and absolutely, Great Books participants are concentrated in the early thirties, although the program does cover a span from the twenties to the seventies. The "significance" of this finding is somewhat difficult to determine, although it may be worth noting that it supports findings later in the analysis that the participants are "busy" people and are not in Great Books to fill in a participation void. The fact that they are clustered moderately in the "busy" years of the life cycle is consistent with this general conclusion.

We are now in a position to ask whether Great Books tends to select people of a particular marital status. Since, in the general population, marital status is correlated with age, sex, and education, it will be necessary to control these variables as best we can. The following table contrasts the per cent married in Great Books with the per cent married among those of the United States population in 1950 who had completed one or more years of college.

The distributions are remarkably similar, considering the small numbers of cases in some of the cells, and we may conclude that the proportion married among the participants does not differ in any important way from the proportion in the general population of "college people." In fact, since

---

[4] Throughout this chapter we will compare Great Books participants with United States Census data for all persons 25 years of age or older who have completed one or more years of college. There are many good reasons why we should not do this (e.g., the participants did not all attend college; our sample is more highly urban than are college people as a whole, etc.), but we feel some comparison is helpful, and this is probably the best yardstick to use, even if it is a rubbery one. Almost all of our sample, after all, have attended college, and college alumni are more urban than the general population; so if we are going to make any comparisons, this seems like the best possibility. For purposes of simplicity, from here on, then, we shall follow the magnanimous example of college development offices and refer to those people with one or more years of college as "alumni" rather than having to say "persons 25 years of age or older in 1950 who reported one or more years of college."

our sampling bias is toward an under-estimate of the proportion married, the program in general probably recruits married people disproportionately.

Regardless of these guesses, our general impression is that "demographically," Great Books participants do not differ in any striking way from the general population of college alumni, and this impression is borne out by Table 7. One would perhaps have hypothesized that the program might attract the retired or the separated, who are at loose ends socially, but this does not appear to be the case.

TABLE 7

Age and Marital Status of First-Year Great Books
Participants and College Alumni
Per cent married

Age	Men		Women	
	U.S. alumni	Great Books	U.S. alumnae	Great Books
25-34	75	72 (215)	78	81 (387)
35-44	89	90 (216)	78	80 (345)
45-54	89	91 (135)	70	75 (201)
55-64	86	85 (47)	56	55 (103)
65+	72	73 (41)	30	36 (52)
		(Base N in parentheses)		

Occupation and Social Status

Since education is one of the best indices of social status in our society, we shall not expect to find any terribly surprising trends when we examine the occupations of the participants. It is clear, already, that we are dealing with an essentially middle-class population.

Table 8 gives us sets of percentages which will enable us to draw our conclusions. It is based on the standard census classification of occupations

TABLE 8

Urban Occupations

Occupation	U.S. 25 and over, 1950			Great Books			
	Total	Male alumni	Female alumnae	Total	Men	Women	Husbands*
Professional	11	39	53	60	65	53	58
Managerial	12	22	6	14	20	6	26
Sales	8	12	5	6	7	4	8
Clerical	12	9	27	16	3	35	3
Blue-collar**	58	18	9	4	5	2	5
	100%	100%	100%	100%	100%	100%	100%
N				1,083	640	434	754
Not working				680	11	669	2
No answer and uncodable				143	41	81	37
				1,906	692	1,184	793

* The occupation of the husband of all women who reported their spouse as the chief wage earner.
** Skilled workers, operatives, household workers, service, and non-farm labor.

but *excludes* farmers and farm workers, as we drew only three such cases in our sample.[5]

The column headed "Total" gives the jobs which were available in 1950. The next two columns tell us that sex and education have a lot to do with who gets the jobs. College alumni, on the whole, get much more desirable jobs, and within the alumni, women tend to move into professions (teaching) and clerical jobs, men into management, professions, and sales.

Now, when we turn to the Great Books participants, we notice an even greater skew. Sixty per cent of those who work are professionals, as contrasted with 11 per cent of the general population. At the bottom of the ladder a smaller per cent of Great Books participants have blue-collar jobs than do the other alumni, 18 per cent of whom are in the blue-collar group.

Now, let us look at the sex distributions in the Great Books sample. When we compare the working women (remembering that they are a minority of women participants) with the job classifications of the female alumnae, we find that the occupational distributions are strikingly similar. Or, to put it conversely, the working alumnae of the U.S. turn up in Great Books about proportionally to the frequency of their jobs in their group. The program may have a little higher "floor" for women, since there are a few less blue-collar workers among the participants, but the slight excess of clerical workers balances it.

For the men, the situation is somewhat different. There is a heavy excess of male professionals in the program and deficits in all other occupational groups, only the managers coming near their fair share.

Why should we get this difference . . . a sex difference in occupations when compared with alumni? We cannot arrive at a definite conclusion, but one hypothesis does suggest itself: it may be that high social status is a necessary condition for joining Great Books. Now, in our society a married woman's social status is generally determined by her husband's occupation, not her own. Thus, the wife of a doctor, who has a high standing in the community, may herself be a nurse, an honored profession which is not, however, high-ranking in terms of social prestige. Likewise, the wife of a corporation executive may be a secretary and still cash in on her husband's job status. We can check this hypothesis by looking at the jobs of the *husbands* of the female participants. If the status hypothesis is true, they should have a very high proportion of high-status jobs and be much like male participants. Looking at the right-hand column of Table 9, we find that the husbands have a lower proportion of professionals than do the male participants, which casts some doubt on the "status" hypothesis.

---

[5] That Great Books is an essentially urban program need not be said. The question is, however, discussed in our introductory discussion of the sampling procedure.

If the situation is not explained by status considerations, it may be that for males alone there is either high selection on the basis of status or that professional males are particularly attracted to the program because of the more "intellectual" nature of their jobs.

There has been, however, a slight fraud at the polls, for 264 of our men have gotten "two votes." The men who participate with their wives appear both among the male participants and among the "husbands."

The following table gives the occupation of the "alternate wage-earner" for the married female participants.

TABLE 9

Occupations of Husbands of Female Participants

Occupational group	Husbands who participate	Husbands who don't participate
Professional	67	53
Managerial	21	28
Sales	7	9
Clerical	1	3
Blue-collar	3	7
N	99% 275	100% 481

There is a statistically significant ($p<.01$) difference between the proportion of professionals in the two groups of husbands. The participating husbands have about the same proportion of professionals as the total group of male participants (67 per cent and 65 per cent), while the non-participating husbands have a lower proportion (53 per cent), which is still higher than that of male alumni (39 per cent). In terms of our two hypotheses, Table 9 suggests the following conclusions:

1) The difference between the participating and non-participating husbands suggests that for the males, occupational values and attitudes may be an important variable in recruitment to Great Books. The professional, whose job is more "intellectual" in some ways, may be more attracted to the program than the "businessman."

2) The difference between the non-participating husbands and the male alumni, and the lack of difference between the women and the female alumnae suggest that occupational values are unimportant for the recruitment of women; but there may be a "social status" variable which tends to bring into the program women whose prestige position is above that of the average female alumna.

Read horizontally instead of vertically, Table 9 also gives us some clues to the mystery of the missing husbands. We find 45 per cent of the professional husbands accompanying their wives; 30 per cent of the manager husbands; and 32 per cent of the salesman husbands. This is entirely consistent with our hunches about the interrelations of sex, status, and occupational values in recruitment. If among males within the upper middle class, occupation is important for recruitment, it follows that women, who are not selected on occupation, but perhaps more on social status, will frequently have businessman husbands who are less attracted to the program. Conversely, the men, most of whom are professionals and of high status, do not meet with a comparable variation among their wives. It should be noted, however, that this is not the whole story, for men as a group still bring along a greater proportion of their spouses (54 per cent) than women married to professionals (45 per cent), although the gap is narrowed considerably.

In short, even controlling crudely for educational levels, Great Books still has a disproportionately strong attraction for the male professional. Likewise, while women do not appear to be selected on the basis of their own jobs, it appears that the husbands of women participants are more likely to be managers and professionals than the average male alumnus.

Social Mobility

Occupational status always has a time dimension, and the question of where a person is now, does not answer the question of where he came from. Status mobility is particularly relevant in any social analysis of a program like Great Books. In a society characterized by relatively frequent mobility as a consequence of a changing occupational structure (the proportion of professionals among employed workers has doubled since 1910), people frequently end up much higher on the social ladder than their starting place. Since Great Books has a heavy proportion of professionals, an occupational group characterized by relatively high upward mobility rates, we may expect to find a considerable number of people who have ascended the ladder. Since, in addition, it would seem that a program like Great Books would be useful for obtaining social and intellectual skills missed during the ascent, it would be interesting to know whether the program tends to attract mobile people in high numbers.

The standard way of assessing mobility is a comparison of the occupation of father and son or father and husband, a path strewn with pitfalls due to the instability of occupations at both ends of the time span and the difficulty of assessing the status of occupations. Since the census does not report such data, the standard reference data come from the 1947 NORC national survey, known as the North-Hatt study.[6] The following table is adapted from that survey.

The trend of the table is clear cut. Great Books participants in high status occupations today are, if anything, considerably less mobile than

---

[6] *Opinion News,* September 1, 1947, pp. 3-13.

the 1947 American cross section. Whether this is because the program attracts less mobile people, or whether their high level of education required fathers who were relatively comfortably fixed, it remains that the "self-made man" and woman are *relatively* rare in our sample, although we do have 286 respondents (ignoring the spouseless women whose current social position is difficult to measure) who have made the transition from farm or blue-collar origins to the upper white-collar regions.

TABLE 10

Mobility

*Per cent whose fathers were skilled, semi-skilled,
service, farm, or labor*

Present Occupation	U.S.a	Great Booksb Males*	Great Booksc Wives*
Professional	42	29 (399)	23 (413)
Managers	56	20 (116)	19 (177)
Sales	53	27 (60)	32 (57)

* Base N in parentheses.
a = Proportion reporting "blue collar or farm" occupation for father for all respondents reporting a given current occupation, regardless of sex.
b = Proportion reporting "blue collar or farm" occupation for father for Great Books male participants reporting a given current occupation.
c = Proportion reporting "blue collar or farm" occupation for father for Great Books married women reporting a given current occupation for their husbands.

In summary: Great Books participants are selected from the upper echelons of the occupational structure, even when compared with American college alumni. Men, in particular, tend disproportionately to be "professionals," [7] possibly because of intrinsic aspects of their jobs. Women tend to be disproportionately recruited from the upper white-collar levels, possibly because of status considerations. In terms of occupational origins, the participants appear less mobile than the general population.

Memberships and Allegiances

In addition to education, family role, and occupation, one's social involvement also consists of a complicated web of formal and informal memberships which reach out beyond the immediate family to the larger social world. Since most of these are analyzed in some detail in the context of "effects of the program" we shall merely sketch out the skeleton here.

Sociability

Among the myths about Great Books participants is the claim that they are ivory towerists who have little or no connections with their community.

---

[7] We have talked about professions at length without mentioning any specific ones. Considering only the respondents' occupations, the following professions each contributed more than 25 respondents: engineers (123); primary and secondary teachers (102); lawyers (61); accountants (39); journalists (36); physicians (34); college teachers (31). These seven groups account for 66 per cent of the professionals; and along with business managers (129) and secretaries (91), account for 59 per cent of the total participants reporting an occupation.

While our chapter on community involvement analyzes this question in some detail, we can here suggest that the myth is incorrect. The following tables probably cover the subject in all the detail it deserves at this point.

TABLE 11

Attachment to the Community

Per cent checking each response in answer to the question,
"What is your emotional feeling about your community?"

Response	Per cent
"I feel I'm a real member of the community . . ."	57
"I do like the community, but I don't feel I'm really a part of it.". .	37
"I rather dislike the community, and I definitely do not feel I'm a part of it."	6
	100%
	N = 1,852

TABLE 12

Number of Civic Organizations to Which Participants Belong[a]

Number of Civic Organizations	Per cent
0	12
1	33
2	25
3 or more	29
	99%
N =	1,505
No answer	404
	1,909

[a] Excluding religious organizations related to a specific congregation, formal civic office, informal sociability groups, and adult education groups.

TABLE 13

Number of Evenings per Month Spent in Informal Visiting and Entertaining

Number of Evenings	Per cent
0	2
1-4	48
5-8	36
9 or more	14
	100%
N =	1,772

In brief, majorities of the respondents report that they feel they are real members of their communities; belong to two or more civic organizations (if we assume that all of the no-answer respondents to this question belong to none, 43 per cent belong to two or more civic organizations) and get together informally more than once a week.

Religion

Since religious readings bulk large in the repertory of the program, it is of interest to note the religious preferences of the participants. Do the "Thomist" readings tend to attract Roman Catholics, or does St. Augustine pull in extra Protestants? Until recently we have had no reliable religious data on a national sample, but a press handout of the Census Bureau in February, 1959, does give the results of a December, 1957, national sample of 35,000 households. Since education is not controlled in the Census report, we had figures from a 1955 NORC national probability sample tabulated for the religious preferences of "alumni" only. The results are summarized in the following table.

TABLE 14

Religious Preference of Great Books Participants

Religion	U.S. Population 14 & Over, 1958	U.S. Alumni, 1955	Great Books Participants
Protestant	66%	72%	62%
Catholic	26	19	10
Jewish	3	4	15
Other	1	1	1
None	3	4	12
	99%	100%	100%
N=			1,752
Uncodable			22
No answer			135
			1,909

Differences between alumni and participants are not pronounced, but certain trends do appear in the table. First, the number reporting "None" is considerably higher in Great Books than among the alumni, who, in turn, are slightly higher than the general population. Second, the proportion of Catholics is lower in Great Books than among the alumni, who are, in turn, lower than the general population. Third, the proportion of Jews is much higher in Great Books than among alumni, who show a slightly greater proportion of Jews than does the general population. Finally, in spite of all these trends, it should be noted the bulk of Great Books participants, as of the other two sample populations, are Protestant.

Now, the reader will remember that there was a heavy concentration of Jews in the largest cities in our sample. Since our sample is biased toward large cities, we have probably overestimated the proportion of Jews in the program and a properly weighted sample would probably bring their proportion down to something more like that of the alumni. This argument, however, works both ways, for Roman Catholics are fairly concentrated in urban areas also. Our guess would be that any sample which eliminated the urban bias would cut the proportion of Roman Catholics too. Balancing all these hypothetical findings together, our inclination would be to advance the hypothesis that if one controls for educational level, the program as a whole may recruit a somewhat lower proportion of Catholics and a higher proportion of "nones," but that other differences in religious preference are probably minimal.

Political Party Preference

Loyalty to a national political party is important for our analysis, both as an index of some basic ideological positions, and in terms of implications about avenues for "social action" which might be affected by participation in Great Books. In the following table, the party preferences of Great Books members are compared with those of the alumni group of the 1955 NORC study [8] and the general United States adult population from the same NORC national sample.

TABLE 15

Party Preference of Great Books Participants

Preference	U.S. Population	Alumni	Great Books
Democratic	51%	36%	48%
Independent	20	26	10
Republican	29	37	41
	100%	99%	99%
N=	2,235	388	1,811

The trends in the above table are far from clear-cut. The proportion of Republicans increases considerably as one moves from the general population to the alumni and slightly as one moves to Great Books. For the other two allegiances, the trend is not straight. Great Books has more Democrats than the alumni and about the same number as the general population; while the program has fewer independents than either comparison sample. To begin with, the proportion of independents may well be a function of question-wording in our study as contrasted to the other survey. If, then, we ignore the independents, we find, among the party-identified, more Democrats in Great Books than among the alumni. There are two reasons for this. First, as we saw in the introduction, our urban bias has probably overestimated the proportion of Democrats in the program as a whole, for in the small towns we find that 32 per cent are Republicans and only 23 per cent in the very large cities. On the other hand, let us examine the relationship between party preference and education. In the following table we see the per cent Democratic by education, for those who reported themselves as either Democrats or Republicans.

---

[8] Jacob J. Feldman, Senior Study Director at NORC, was a helpful consultant for these tabulations, as he has been throughout the course of our study.

TABLE 16

Education and Party Preference of Great Books Participants

Education	Per cent Democratic	N*
Less than high school	52	(40)
High school	50	(141)
Post high, non-college	48	(100)
Part college	43	(408)
Bachelor's	44	(403)
Some graduate work	46	(266)
Master's degree	53	(193)
Other graduate degree	55	(92)
Ph.D.	62	(98)

* Base N in parentheses.

The relationship appears to be "curvilinear." That is, the proportion of Democrats declines steadily as one moves toward the middle of the educational scale from either extreme. Now, compared to the general population Great Books has fewer less-educated people, but it has many more highly educated people. The Democrats it loses at the bottom, it may regain at the top. Thus, we doubt that, even if a less biased sample raised the proportion of Republicans, it would put them into an overwhelming majority.

In short, the only hypothesis we would hazard is that a compensating process may be at work. The high status level of Great Books participants may raise the proportion of Republicans in comparison with the general population, or even in comparison with alumni. At the same time the disproportionate number of people with graduate training may insure that a fair proportion of Democrats are attracted. The net result of these two tendencies may be to keep a fairly equal balance between adherents of the two parties.

Summary

What are the participants like? They tend to be highly educated, quite married, somewhat female, disproportionately professional men and wives of white collar husbands; infrequently "intellectuals"; under-mobile; possibly disproportionately irreligious; possibly under-proportionally Catholic; sociable; joining Republicans and Democrats.

Where participants can be compared with the national population of college alumni, they tend to accentuate those qualities (mostly associated with high levels of interest and intellectual sophistication) which, in turn, differentiate the alumni from the general population.

In short, the participants are well-educated, high-status, socially active, youngish adults.

Let us, however, note two things which they are not:

First, our evidence suggests that they are not, despite their high level of education and later data on their intellectual abilities, so immersed in ideas and culture that these have become the center of their lives. The stereotype of the bookish, ivory tower intellectual, does not apply to these people, most of whom share basic middle-class values and few of whom consider themselves intellectuals. The creative intellectual professions are rare among them, and ties to the world of civic organization and political party are strong.

Second, our evidence suggests that they are not, relative to their society, men and women of high power and influence. A very few "elite" Great Books groups have created the impression that this program reaches into the Olympian heights of money and power in this country. Our data do not support this idea. In the first place, only one out of our 1,909 respondents is a nationally known figure, and that person is in the field of entertainment. In the second place, given a national social structure in which the sources of influence and power are disproportionately concentrated among male businessmen, the tendency for the respondents to be women or male professionals means that few of them are located in the places in the social structure where key community or national decisions are made. In fairness, we should note that relative to the general population, Great Books participants are extremely highly selected in terms of prestige and ability. At the same time, when one considers, as we will throughout this analysis, the ramifications of Great Books experience in the social worlds of the participants, we must bear in mind that the participants tend to be an elite of talent, technical skill, and intellectual training, not an elite of persons in key decision-making positions in their community and society.

Part B

SELF-ASSESSMENTS

CHAPTER ONE

SELF-ASSESSMENTS

In Part A of this report we sketched a picture of the participants in our sample, building a composite impression from tabulations of their salient characteristics. Without going any further, we could guess that they have strong intellectual interests, have fairly high motivations toward group participation, and are not using Great Books as a vehicle for gaining social polish. These are, however, inferences from our static portrait. In order to get a more nearly accurate picture, in Part B we shall summarize our findings on the respondents' own reports on their reasons for joining the program and then examine, as the first of our assessments of effects, their own statements on what they have gained from being in Great Books.

What Do They Want from the Program?

What do they want from the program? Probably the most important aspect of this question is that we need to ask it. Unlike a course in business

English, French cooking, or arc welding, the purposes of an adult program in liberal education are not explicit. Proponents of such programs believe strongly that adult liberal education has purpose and consequence, but these cannot be laid out in a neat outline fashion. To begin with, a good case can be made that the purpose of liberal education is liberal education, not life adjustment or social amelioration. At the same time, it is also firmly believed that the liberally educated man finds his education applicable in all the areas of his life.

One assumption with which we can start is that, for different people, the program will have different purposes. While the content of the readings and the pattern of discussion are a "constant," the needs and life experiences which the members bring to the program are probably the most important factor in determining what purposes they see in it. People come into Great Books with motivations ranging from speed reading to solutions of world problems, and one of the working assumptions of Great Books is that the curriculum and discussion are rich enough and broad enough to meet a great variety of motivations.

Therefore, our approach was to ask the participants what they wanted from the program. On the second page of our questionnaire we listed 23 specific motivations, based on our impressions from pilot studies and conferences with administrators in Great Books and The Fund for Adult Education.

We can begin by looking at the frequency distribution. Right away we notice two characteristics of Table 17, following.

First, motivations other than those included in the list are seldom volunteered by the respondents (10 per cent volunteered an "other" reason). Now, it is never fair to compare the volume of "write-ins" with those items which are listed in a questionnaire, but, in this case, the comparison does seem to warrant the belief that there is probably no really important or frequent motive which is not tapped by our list.

Second, we notice that only one item on the list was checked by a majority, and the bulk were checked by between 10 and 30 per cent. This suggests that our hunch about diversified motivations was probably correct.

Diversity, however, is accompanied by some degree of overlap. The motivations are not mutually exclusive, and the participants tended to check fairly high numbers of motives; 93 per cent checked more than one, and 51 per cent checked six or more.

This, in turn, suggests that our approach should consider "complexes" of motives, rather than discrete "reasons."

TABLE 17

Reasons for Joining Great Books

Per cent of respondents checking each purpose as something they "definitely had in mind as a reason for joining—regardless of whether or not Great Books met this expectation."

Rank	Reason	Per cent Checking [1]
1)	To learn what the greatest minds in history have to say abobut the basic issues of life	64
2)	Reacquainting myself with a cultural background which had become rusty	44
3)	Improving my ability to analyze and criticize arguments	42
4)	Escaping the intellectual narrowness of my occupation	42
5)	Talking with people who have more intellectual interests than my usual "social" friends	40
6)	Improving my reading skills	32
7)	Getting a chance to express ideas I had been thinking and reading about	30
8)	Escaping the intellectual narrowness of being a housewife	30
9)	Improving my taste in fiction and poetry	24
10)	Making new friends	24
11)	Gaining insight into myself and my personal problems	24
12)	Escaping the intellectual narrowness of my community	23
13)	Becoming more sure of myself when talking with people of higher intellectual background	21
14)	Supplementing an unduly narrow or technical college training	21
15)	Gaining a better intellectual background for my participation in community organizations and community affairs	19
16)	Developing common interests with my spouse	18
17)	Becoming a more effective participant in group discussions outside of Great Books	17
18)	Meeting people who are quite different from me	16
19)	Finding solutions to contemporary problems	15
20)	Other (any specific "write in")	10
21)	Improving my ability to carry out my job through the intellectual training of reading Great Books	10
22)	Increasing my ability to carry out my job through improving my ability to participate in group discussions	8
23)	Developing the ability to lead group discussions outside of Great Books	8
24)	Gaining the equivalent of a college education	7

[1] N = 1,904.

Cluster Analysis

The statistical method we used to analyze the data on motivations is called "cluster analysis." [2] The procedure involves computing the inter-correlations of all possible pairs of items.[3]

The full details of the cluster analysis are reported at length in our original write-up (including a very scientific-looking matrix of 264 inter-correlations). The upshot, however, is fairly simple. The statistical patterns

---

[2] Cf. Robert C. Tryon, *Cluster Analysis* (Ann Arbor, Michigan: Edwards Bros., 1939).
[3] For the technical reader, we may note that we used "Q" measures of association rather than correlation coefficients in our analysis. Since the technique is essentially "non-parametric" in its logic, we feel no real need to apologize except that the use of non-parametric measures in factor-analysis-type research seems to be an affect-producing activity.

suggested that the twenty-three motives could be thought of as bunched into four clusters, plus seven sort of "lone-wolf" motives which don't have very strong relationships with the rest. We shall discuss each of the four clusters and then turn to the problem of finding out what sorts of people express what sorts of motivation.

Cluster A — "Stepping Stone"

The tightest cluster is A, which is made up of the following:

23. Developing the ability to lead group discussions outside of Great Books.
21. Improving my ability to carry out my job through the intellectual training of reading Great Books.
22. Increasing my ability to carry out my job through improving my ability to participate in group discussions.
17. Becoming a more effective participant in group discussions outside of Great Books.

What these seem to have in common is a focus on the job and on group discussions outside of the program. Now, we should note that Number 4 (Escaping the intellectual narrowness of my occupation) and Number 10 (Making friends) have quite low relationships with this cluster, so the issue does not seem to be "job" or "groupyness" *per se*. Rather, it appears to us that what these four motives have in common is a focus on learning specific techniques in Great Books that can be used as a stepping stone for success in other areas. The focus is not intellectual ("Learning what the great minds have to say" has a low relationship with this group), but rather on specific skills and techniques, and — we hate to say it — gimmicks. Cluster A appears to be highly pragmatic. It is also relatively infrequent, containing only motives of rank 17 or lower.

Cluster B — "Content"

The four motives in Cluster B are:

1. To learn what the greatest minds in history have to say about the basic issues of life.
11. Gaining insight into myself and my personal problems.
15. Gaining a better intellectual background for my participation in community organizations and community affairs.
19. Finding solutions to contemporary problems.

We have called this cluster "Content" because it seems to focus on the content of the books, and excludes group participation as a means or end. It does involve areas outside the immediate program, like "Stepping Stone," but these are quite intellectual and abstract, definitely not gimmicks. One might think of the "Content" cluster as the official motivation for the program. In its general aspect, motive 1, it is the most common reason; and in its applied areas (self, community, and world) it includes less frequent motives, but not the rare ones which are included in "Stepping Stone."

Cluster C — "Self-Help"

Cluster C includes:

6. Improving my reading skills.
9. Improving my taste in fiction and poetry.
13. Becoming more sure of myself when talking with people of higher intellectual background.
24. Gaining the equivalent of a college education.

One needs little ingenuity to figure out what underlies Cluster C. It is what a nameless consultant to the study calls "They Laughed when I sat down at the piano, but were they surprised when I began to talk about Plato!", and we have decided to call it "Self-Help." It requires little comment, except to say that it does not include group participation in any form, and its elements have a wide range of frequency, being roughly less frequent as the aims appear more ambitious.

Cluster D — "Cosmopolitanism"

Cluster D is made up of:

5. Talking with people who have more intellectual interests than my usual "social" friends.
12. Escaping the intellectual narrowness of my community.
18. Meeting people who are quite different from me.

Cluster D is made up of pushes and pulls. The push, apparently, is supplied by feelings of boredom and narrowness in the social world of the participants, while the pull is the hope that in the program one can find people who are more alert and intellectual. The elements here are both "social," since meeting people seems to be the cure, and "intellectual," since the lack thereof appears to be the cause. We felt that "Cosmopolitanism" came pretty close to expressing the theme. Like the "Content" cluster, it includes one high-ranking motive and others that are less common.

The remaining lone-wolf motives (2, 4, 7, 8, 10, 14, 16) seem straightforward, and require no further discussion.[4]

These, then, are the clusters of motives we find in our data: 1) "Stepping Stone"; 2) "Content"; 3) "Self-Help"; and 4) "Cosmopolitanism." If you

---

[4] An exception: It seems to us that *a priori*, "Escaping the intellectual narrowness of being a housewife" should belong in "Cosmopolitanism." It just doesn't, and we found no good way to explain this.

squint a bit intellectually, each appears to have a reasonable psychological unity, and the statistical pattern is fairly respectable, at least from our experience with cluster analyses. We should, however, note two qualifications:

1) These are the clusters of the things we asked about. No doubt, if we had asked different questions, or even slightly different questions, we might have gotten different clusters.

2) The clusters are based on what people *say* motivated them, not necessarily what *really* did. Our general impression throughout the survey was that almost all of the respondents tried very hard to tell us the truth, but the human animal has a vast capacity to kid himself and make himself appear in a good light. What *really* motivates these people is probably beyond the capacity of survey research to measure, but we should also remember that, for many purposes, conscious and overt motives can be as important as those tucked away in the depth of the unconscious.

How frequent are these motivational clusters in our sample of participants? No clear answer seems possible. If we examine the frequency of the individual items in the clusters, we see a wide range of ranks in Table 17, with the exception of "Stepping Stone," which only includes items of rank 17 or below. Frequency seems related more to the specificity of the motive than to its content. Clusters B, C, and D each include specific motives which are among the first five in the rank order, and we suspect that if we had written a very general item in the style of Cluster A, it might have drawn a much higher number of responses.

The closest we can come to an estimate is to calculate for each cluster the number of persons who checked at least one of the motives in it.

TABLE 18

Per Cent of Respondents Checking for Each Cluster at Least One Motive

Cluster	N = 1,904	Per cent
B) Content		71
D) Cosmopolitanism		68
C) Self-Help		51
A) Stepping Stone		28

By this very rough criterion, "Content" and "Cosmopolitanism" appear to be quite frequent, slightly more than two-thirds of the sample mentioning at least one of the constituent items. "Self-Help" splits the group in half, 51 per cent mentioning one of the motives, 49 per cent not doing so. "Stepping Stone," as the ranks of its specific motives suggest, is quite infrequent.

In the next section of this chapter, we shall switch from the question of absolute frequency to that of relative frequency among different subgroups of participants.

Subgroup Differences in Motivations

Many of the motives in our list are quite specific and by definition can be found concentrated in a few subgroups in the sample. Thus, it wouldn't tax our IBM machines much to find out that there is a relationship between "Escaping the intellectual narrowness of being a housewife" and sex and marital status. (About 35 per cent of the sample are housewives and 30 per cent of the sample checked this item.) For our more abstract clusters, however, the patterns do not appear to be obvious. Therefore, we examined the statistical relationships between "checking one or more items in a given cluster" and selected social characteristics of the respondents. We shall consider each of our four motivational clusters in turn.

"Content"

The answer for "Content" is clear . . . very clear, for it doesn't correlate with anything at all. Actually, there are a few trends: 67 per cent of the infrequent church attenders and 74 per cent of the frequent attenders check at least one "Content" item; the corresponding proportion for "no college" is 68 per cent; for those with graduate training, 72 per cent; for men, 68 per cent; and for women, 73 per cent.

"Content" also has a slight, but fairly consistent relationship with type of community. It was mentioned by 64 per cent in the very big cities; 70 per cent in the suburbs as a whole; 74 per cent in the big cities; and 76 per cent in the small towns. Again, we would predict that the correct weighting of our cases by type of community would raise the over-all total checking "Content," although it is equally true that, regardless of the size of the community, "Content" is mentioned by two-thirds or more of the participants, and there is no type of community where it is a "minority" motivation.

Now, while extended statistical magic might produce a few serviceable tables (since women have lower educational levels than men, controlling education would undoubtedly produce a sex difference in favor of the women) the most meaningful conclusion is that in any subgroup created by dividing the participants in terms of age, education, sex, religion, years in the program, scores on measures of intellectual ability, political party preference, etc., etc., one will find very close to 70 per cent mentioning a "Content" motivation.

Now, while candor forces us to admit that if correlations had turned up, we probably could have made good sense out of them, when we turn on our "retrospectoscope" we find that this is not at all surprising. Presumably, "Content" is the basic motivation of the vast bulk of the participants, and there is no reason why, *within* Great Books, single females or Democrats or Roman Catholics should be more interested or less interested in Great Books in a literal sense. Now, of course, subgroups may be expected to vary to a great extent in what they believe the Great Books say and in terms of how they use the content they get, but we still remain unperturbed when we are forced to conclude that interest in the Great Books is spread lavishly and randomly throughout the participants, particularly when we remember that failure to check items in the "Content" cluster does not indicate *dis*interest in "Content," but rather that this was not one of the salient motivations for entering the program.

"Self-Help"

The pattern for the "Self-Help" cluster is equally clear, but instead of no correlations, we find a whole bundle of them. The self-helper is more likely to be found among: women, those born in the United States, Catholics, those from families whose bread-winner has a lower occupational status, respondents with low scores on a test of knowledge of the liberal arts, Republicans, those who think of themselves as "serious minded" or "lowbrow," and those with lower levels of formal education.

We should note that there are also a few characteristics that show little relationship to "Self-Help" as a motive. Among them: frequency of church attendance, age, and intention to continue in the program next year.

In spite of the wide variety in the apparent nature of the characteristics which correlate with the "Self-Help" cluster, most of them are direct or indirect measures of intellectual training and ability. If so, the point is that the people who want intellectual self-help are the people who need it.

In order to check our impression that intellectual training or ability is the important variable underlying the "Self-Help" motivation, we reexamined all the original relationships, controlling for education and years of exposure. We chose education as our "quality" variable for three reasons: 1) it is probably quite reliably measured; 2) it is a powerful correlate of all the other measures of intellectual ability; and 3) unlike the test scores, it is known by the participant and hence is more likely to influence his conscious motivations. In order to avoid getting entangled in the "dropout" problem, we will consider only first year participants here.[5]

When we apply education as a control, what happens is that the "social" variables, on the whole tend to evaporate, while the more overtly "intellectual" measures tend to remain related to "Self-Help."

---

[5] Examination of the full tables shows the same trends in general in the advanced years, except that, as is generally true in our analysis, "demographic" relationships are reduced in the advanced years, presumably because program experience tends to "over-ride" initial social differences as time goes on.

One social difference, however, does not fade away when we divide the participants by educational level. This is "generation" or nativity, and it is interesting to note that this is about the only place in our entire survey where this measure has any important relationship with any aspect of Great Books.[6]

We classified the respondents as first-, second-, third-, or fourth-generation, depending on whether they, their parents, their grandparents, or none of these were foreign-born. The following table contrasts first-generation, second-generation, and those with one foreign-born parent, with all others of longer historical ties to this country. Since "Self-Help" is less frequently reported in the advanced years, either because self-helpers drop out or because more are being recruited each year, we shall consider first-year participants only.

TABLE 19

Generation and "Self-Help," Controlling Education and Exposure

Per cent high on "Self-Help"

Years of Great Books completed	Education	Older Americans	Newer Americans
0	No college	77 (65)	65 (52)
	Part college and A.B.	64 (238)	54 (93)
	Graduate study	41 (172)	35 (78)
	(Base N in parentheses)		

There is a distinct tendency for "Older Americans" to be higher on "Self-Help" than "Newer Americans." We think that what Table 19 really tells us is something about the nature of the "Newer Americans" in Great Books rather than about "self-helpers." They are not the culturally under-privileged (35 per cent in the first year have graduate training, as compared with 36 per cent of the older Americans) one associates with the term "first- and second-generation." Just as the entire group does not appear highly mobile occupationally, as we noted above, our guess would be that "Newer Americans" are recruited not from those seeking "Americanization," but from those who come from cultural backgrounds superior to that of "Older Americans."

In summary, the social subgroups differ quite a bit in the relative proportions of members who are motivated by needs in the "Self-Help" cluster. Further analysis, however, indicates that, with the single exception of "generation" (which we think reflects early cultural background, not "ethnic differences"), all these differences are due to differences in level of formal education.

---

[6] There is one exception: Our measure of "classical music sophistication," which is one of the workhorses in Part C, shows a definitely higher level of musical familiarity among the newer Americans, which is consistent with our conclusions in the following paragraphs. Music, although important in our statistical analysis, is, however, peripheral from the viewpoint of the program.

"Cosmopolitanism"

Who are the "Cosmopolitans," or would-be "Cosmopolitans," the people who want to escape intellectual narrowness through meeting more stimulating people? They tend to be 1) youngish; 2) of high occupational status; 3) high education; 4) Republicans; and 5) from small towns. However, this list is somewhat deceptive as we shall see when we turn to the "partials."

In the first place, age washes out education, one of the few times in our survey where education is elbowed aside by a crass demographic variable.

TABLE 20

Education and "Cosmopolitanism," Controlling Age
Per cent high on "Cosmopolitanism"

Age	No College	Part College & A.B.	Graduate Work
		Education	
Under 34	75 (64)	73 (352)	73 (239)
35-44	71 (92)	66 (256)	79 (223)
45+	58 (134)	62 (229)	59 (213)
	(Base N in parentheses)		

In spite of the fact that there is a slight but steady increase of "Cosmopolitanism" with education (from 66 to 71 per cent) in the general group, within an age bracket there is no consistent pattern, there being a fairly strong negative relationship between age and education (as there is in the general U.S. population). Within each educational group, however, the participants who are 45 years old and over are definitely lower, and the 35-44 somewhat lower, than the tads under 34 years of age.

A similar analysis indicates that occupational prestige is also a spurious correlate, the more highly educated people having better jobs. The following table, however, summarizes the contributions of the three variables which do seem to relate to cosmopolitanism.

TABLE 21

Age, Party Preference, Type of Community, and "Cosmopolitanism"
Per cent high on "Cosmopolitanism"

Community	Party	Under 35	35-44	45 or more
			Age	
Very large and large city	D	70 (141)	67 (142)	55 (138)
	R	70 (90)	71 (63)	61 (87)
Suburbs	D	71 (129)	74 (92)	53 (81)
	R	73 (111)	73 (116)	64 (118)
Small town	D	79 (33)	73 (37)	60 (25)
	R	81 (32)	89 (44)	74 (50)
		(Base N in parentheses)		

All three characteristics appear to contribute to "Cosmopolitanism." In each of the six rows the group under 35 is higher on "Cosmopolitanism" than the over 45s, and in four out of the six the 35-44s are in the middle. With only one small exception (35-44 in the suburbs) Republicans are more interested in "Cosmopolitanism" than Democrats, even when one controls for age and city size. both of which are related to party preference. Likewise, in each case the small town participant is more likely to report this motive than the person from the big city, and the suburbanite tends to fall between them.

The three variables jointly produce a range from 55 per cent high among older, big city Democrats to more than 80 per cent among young, small town Republicans, although we should note that in every cell in the table, "Cosmopolitanism" is in the majority. There is no subgroup which is "low" on this motivation, but they do differ in how high they are.

The relationship with city size appears obvious, the need for "Cosmopolitanism" decreasing with the cosmopolitanism of the community. (We should make clear, for the record, that we named this cluster *before* we knew of this correlation.) Likewise, the fact that younger people are higher seems reasonable either because of their generally higher interest in new stimuli or the fact that their social worlds are less structured and they are more "ready" to find the new friends which are the cure defined in the cluster.

What is somewhat interesting, however, is that, of the three, probably party preference is the strongest predictor, in the sense that it shows the fewest and smallest exceptions in the table. Now, we do have some evidence that Republicanism is associated with social conservatism in our sample and in the general population. However, the failure of social status or frequency of church attendance to correlate here suggests that this is a blind alley, since both of these are also indices of social conservatism. Although we have had to wrestle with it to wring out any coherent interpretations, one of the striking aspects of these data is the frequency with which political preference is related to intellectual interests and orientations, independent of the background variables of education and social status. We shall see much more of the same in Part C.

"Stepping Stone"

The motivations we have called "Stepping Stone" revolve around the aim of learning techniques which can be applied in specific areas outside of Great Books. These are, as we noted, rather infrequent among the program's participants. Further analysis shows that, like "Self-Help," and unlike "Content" or "Cosmopolitanism," "Stepping Stone" is reported less frequently in the advanced years — a situation which hints that it may be associated with dropping out of the program.

In terms of its subgroup associations, we find these aims more common among: a) those with weaker ties to the family and b) highly educated people in lower status jobs. We shall consider only first year participants here.

Among the men this motive is more common among the single males (the number of cases is too small in the high status group to repeat the comparison there). Among the women, working wives tend to be higher than housewives in both status levels, and in the low status level (the only place we have a reasonable number of cases) non-married women are even higher. Despite the small number of cases in crucial cells, the variable does not appear to reflect "working" *per se,* for just as many married men work as single men, and the wives are about as frequently employed as the non-married women. Rather, Table 22 suggests that "family responsibilities" may be a variable. Those who are most tied to their own families and homes appear least interested in the program as a "Stepping Stone" to success in the occupational and organizational world. We also notice, among the married men and housewives, a status difference; those who already have good jobs or are married to men with good jobs being less interested in this motive. The following table gives further detail on this variable.

TABLE 22

Life Cycle Role and "Stepping Stone" (First Year Participants)

Per cent high on "Stepping Stone"

Status	Men			Women	
	Married	Single	Housewives	Working Wives	Single & Ex-Married
Low	40 (101)	50 (26)	32 (123)	38 (48)	43 (96)
High	28 (86)	— (12)	23 (120)	42 (26)	— (6)
		(Base N in parentheses)			

TABLE 23

Status, Education, and "Stepping Stone"

Per cent high on "Stepping Stone"

Status	Education		
	No college	Part College & A.B.	Graduate Work
High	50 (20)	29 (112)	29 (125)
Low	29 (89)	39 (204)	44 (110)
	(Base N in parentheses)		

Table 23 helps us to specify the status relationship a little. We find that the status difference varies with the respondent's educational level. Among the no-college group there is no status difference, among the middle educational group there is a moderate difference, and among the graduate group, a high difference. This suggests that the "Stepping Stone" aspiration is concentrated among those with high education, but less prestigeful jobs, a group which may be assumed to have both a high drive for advancement in job and community and sufficient intellectual background not to feel threatened by Great Books as too difficult.

Summary

What do the participants want out of Great Books? Different people seem to want different things, and most people seem to want several things. Therefore, we can think of the motives as being varied and complex.

Statistical analysis of the motivations reported by the participants indicated that we could think of four major clusters of motives which tend to be internally correlated but weakly related to other clusters. We gave the four the names of: 1) "Content," "2) "Self-Help," 3) "Cosmopolitanism," and 4) "Stepping Stone," to indicate our impression that they involved: 1) interest in the content of the readings, 2) desire to make up for deficits in cultural background, 3) hopes of meeting intellectual people in order to escape a dull community or social world, and 4) aims of learning specific skills to apply in job or community organization. In terms of frequency, "Content" and "Cosmopolitanism" (in one or another of their specific motive forms) seem characteristic motives of most of the group; "Self-Help" is sought by about one-half; and only a few see Great Books as a "Stepping Stone."

We also explored differences in the motivations of specific social subgroups and categories within the sample. Although correlations turned up, our general impression is that, except for "Self-Help" the differences are not terribly important. Every type of motive is found in every type of participant, and the differences we find are those of emphasis and shading. When we also consider that people tend to report multiple rather than single motivations, we would be hard put to find social groups or categories that have radically different motivations up and down the line. The odds are pretty much that, as they sit around the table, in spite of any differences in sex, job, religion, age, generation, etc., most of the people will be talking with others who have pretty much the same aims, and very seldom will they be talking across the table to someone who has a radically different conception of the purposes of the program.

CHAPTER TWO

What Do They Say They Get from the Program?

In a sense, all of the remaining pages of this report are devoted to answers to the question, "What do the participants get from participating in Great Books?" Part C of the report, which follows this chapter, is devoted to the analysis of participants' scores on certain tests and statistical measures which attempt to assess effects. In this chapter, however, the data consist of the participants' own beliefs about the effects of participation.

From a technical point of view the materials reported here are neither "objective" nor "valid" in the sense that thermometers are objective and valid measures of temperature. Presumably, very few of the respondents would stay in the program if they didn't believe it had some effect, and fewer yet would care to put themselves in the dilemma of saying that they loved Great Books but weren't getting anything out of it. We feel, however, that both types of evidence are necessary for a full understanding of the program. In the first place, as we have already seen, the motivations of the members are diverse and complex and, unlike many programs, the aims of the Great Books program are really defined by the motivations of the participants. If such be the case, it seems reasonable to see how the participants evaluate their success in meeting the goals they have described. In the second place, since Great Books is a totally voluntary organization, its continuance is dependent on the belief of its members — whether correct or not — that it is a worthwhile organization. Lastly, ignoring the absolute "level" of effects reported, a comparison of subgroups which are relatively high and low on reported effects may yield information about the differential impact of participation for different groups.

This chapter is divided into two parts. In the first part, we shall examine the "general impact" of the program. In the second, we shall look again at the 23 specific motivations described in the preceding chapter. Previously we looked at the 23 items as *motivations* for joining the program. Now we shall look at these same items but in terms of whether the respondent feels them to be an *effect* of participation in the program.

Impact

Toward the end of our questionnaire, we asked the following:

"On the whole, which of the following best describes your feeling about Great Books?"

The distribution of responses is as follows:

TABLE 24

Impact

Answer	Per cent	N
It is a marvelous program and has had a genuine impact on me	42	762
It is a fine thing and I enjoy it very much, but I can't say it has changed me very much	55	987
I have enjoyed some parts of it, but on the whole I haven't gotten much out of it	3	56
I haven't gotten anything at all out of Great Books	0	0
	100	1,805
Not a member, just visiting		11
No answer		93
		1,909

The sampled participants do not appear to be a sullen and disappointed group. Nearly half of them claim that the program has had "a genuine impact," and not a single one said that he had gotten nothing at all out of Great Books! Our impact thermometer seems to be graded only from high to extremely high. Clearly, the participants are pleased with the program. Nevertheless, we must note the following qualification. Unlike almost anything else which is of serious educational intent, Great Books is deliberately very low in paraphernalia which would tend to bind the less-than-enthusiastic member. There is no tuition, no certificate of accomplishment, no degree, no teacher, no monitor to take attendance, and no fixed terminal date. Thus, for the person who dislikes either the readings or the group or both, there is absolutely nothing to keep him in the program. It may be, then, that the program contains no sizable group of less-than-enthusiasts, not only because it creates high levels of enthusiasm, but also because it loses the non-enthusiast completely.

One cleavage is apparent, however. While everyone believes that the program is a fine thing, the respondents can be divided into 42 per cent who claim that it has "had a genuine impact on me" and 58 per cent of equally admiring ones who, nevertheless, do not report that they have been changed much. We shall call the first "high impact" and the latter "low impact." Thus, what began as a measure of degree of favorableness toward the program turned out to discriminate only between high and low impact groups in a sample which is almost 100 per cent favorable.

Who are the people who report high impact?

The two best predictors are the respondent's level of formal education and his number of years of exposure to the program.

TABLE 25

Education, Exposure, and Impact

Per cent reporting high impact

Years Completed	Less Than College Graduate	College Graduate
0	40 (265)	21 (398)
1 and 2	55 (206)	36 (343)
3 or more	69 (167)	56 (255)
(Base N in parentheses)		

Both factors contribute to impact, resulting in a range from 21 per cent among the first year college graduates to 69 per cent among the advanced year non-graduates. We notice, too, that impact starts early, nearly half reporting impact in the first year, non-college group, and increases steadily with years of exposure. Whether this is due to increasing impact with increased exposure, or to a tendency for the low impact group to leave the program, we do not know.

Education is also an elusive problem. To begin with, the "zero order" data suggest that the determinant is not the "degree" thereof but the presence or absence of the bachelor's degree.

TABLE 26

Education and Impact

Per cent reporting high impact

Education	Per cent	N
No college	52	(280)
Part college	52	(411)
Bachelor's	35	(402)
Graduate work	36	(663)

The foregoing table suggests that education here may be an index of self-definition rather than a measure of pure intellectual ability and training.

By and large, the sort of "social categories" which we considered in Part A are unimportant for impact. Religious preference, party preference, sex, marital status, type of community, frequency of church attendance, etc., have no consistent pattern of relationship with impact when education and years of exposure have been controlled. Two variables, however, do show some relationship. They are age, and prestige of the occupation of the head of the household. Younger people and high status people are a little less likely to report high impact, even controlling for education.

We would suggest the following: The fact that older people, less educated people, and lower status people tend to report higher impact suggests that the major variable in impact is the contrast between the cultural stimulation of the program and the intellectual stimulation of the respondent's natural habitat. Many surveys have shown that younger people, higher status people, and highly educated people tend disproportionately to read, to be well informed, to be up on things, and to have wider contacts.

Another way of saying much the same thing is to note that "Content" type variables have little to do with impact. Although specific content — like, say, Thomism — is an important part of the readings, Protestants, Catholics, Jews, and non-religionists are about equally likely to report high impact. Again political philosophy is important in the readings, but people of all ideological leanings report high impact. In short, we would guess that what gives the program its "impact" is its general purpose of exposure to intellectual materials, and that specific issues, values, positions, and prejudices have little to do with differences in impact. By and large, the people who report high impact are those for whom we may expect that the program presents the greatest contrast with their everyday situation, regardless of the specific content involved.

If social characteristics affect impact, what about motivations? In a way they do, and in a way they don't. What seems to be important is the *number* of motivations checked, not their specific content. The following table shows the relationship between motivations and impact, controlling for exposure and education.

TABLE 27

Number of Motivations and Impact, Controlling Education and Exposure

Per cent high impact

| Exposure (years) | Education | Number of Motives Checked | | |
		0-3	4-6	7 or more
0	A.B. or more	14 (73)	21 (161)	24 (163)
	Less than A.B.	24 (50)	41 (92)	47 (122)
1 & 2	A.B. or more	33 (95)	32 (130)	43 (118)
	Less than A.B.	50 (54)	56 (78)	58 (73)
3 or more	A.B. or more	42 (79)	61 (104)	65 (72)
	Less than A.B.	68 (54)	65 (57)	72 (56)

(Base N in parentheses)

The proportion reporting high impact increases steadily, within an educational and exposure group, with the number of motivations reported. Therefore, we conclude that the more the participant wants from the program the more likely he is to report that the program has had a genuine impact on him.

Is the program, then, a sort of giant ink blot onto which the participants project their needs and desires, or does the program itself have any effects independent of the motivations of the individual members? Before we leap to a conclusion, let us turn to the analysis of specific motives.

Specific Effects

So far we have talked about the effects of the program simply in terms of "impact," a generalized sort of effect which can be thought of as the result of a large number of different consequences of participating in Great Books. Since, as we must continually stress, motivations are multiple and heterogeneous, it is possible for a person to report "high impact," but to deny that one or another specific "effect" happened to him. Likewise, low impact can conceal a number of very definite and specific changes if they are outweighed by other areas where there is no change. Thus, a full understanding of subjective effects requires that we shift from the global level of impact to a consideration of concrete instances.

The data on motivations, you will remember, came from a check list on the second page of the questionnaire. On the same page was a second question, which read as follows:

"In the right hand column, please place a check by any of the items which you think has definitely been an effect of Great Books for you — regardless of whether or not it was a reason for joining."

We shall now examine our same 23 items, this time from the perspective of effects, instead of motivations. Motivations, however, cannot be avoided, for the first thing we notice is that the proportion reporting a given effect is to a large degree a function of two familiar factors: 1) motivation, and 2) exposure. Here, for example, is the per cent reporting "Escaping the intellectual narrowness of my community" as an effect, tabulated by exposure and motivation.

TABLE 28

Motivation, Exposure, and "Escaping the Intellectual Narrowness of My Community"

Per cent reporting as an effect *of participation*

Exposure (years)	Checked "Escaping Community" as Reason for Joining	Did not check "Escaping Community" as Reason for Joining
0	44 (157)	1 (586)
1 & 2	53 (140)	13 (433)
3 or more	74 (106)	21 (345)
	(Base N in parentheses)	

The differences are very strong, in both ways. For both the motivated and the non-motivated, the proportion reporting the effect zooms with exposure, but within each exposure group there are striking differences by degree of motivation. Thus, among those who did not check it as a reason for joining, 21 times as many report it as an effect in the advanced years as in the first, but in the first year the "motivated" are 44 times as likely to report it as the non-motivated!

The same pattern, in general, holds for each of the 23 motivations. The question is, however, whether the motivation effect is "additive" or not. What we mean is this. Let us think of the proportion saying "X is an effect" as a function of two things: one, the true effectiveness of the program in that area, the other, the degree of motivation of the participant. If the motivation effect is "additive" it will raise the effect proportion of each item the same amount. If, on the other hand, it is not so, motivation may raise the effect proportion of some items considerably and raise the effect proportion of others only a little.

The check on this is to look at the correlation between the effect proportions for the motivated and non-motivated for each of the 23 items. If motivation is additive, there should be a strong linear correlation. If not, the correlation should be lessened and/or curvilinear. Table 29 shows the correlation for the zero-years-of-exposure group. It can be read as follows. Each dot tells the proportion reporting this item [1] as an effect, for the motivated and for the non-motivated (i.e., people who did and did not check it as a reason for joining). Thus, for item 7 (Getting a chance to express ideas) 67 per cent of the motivated and 22 per cent of the non-motivated checked it as an effect.

Let us now examine the table in detail. In the first place, the diagonal line running from the lower left to the upper right gives us the locations of all points where the proportion reporting the effect in the motivated and non-motivated is identical. Since all the entries are above this line, we can conclude that motivation makes a big difference. There is no single case where the proportion reporting the effect among the non-motivated comes close to the proportion among the motivated.

What about the correlation? The pattern is not random, for items which tend to be low for the motivated are also low for the non-motivated, and the items which are very high for one are also very high for the other. The relationship, however, appears to be asymmetrical (curvilinear). Items which rank high for the non-motivated also tend to be high for the motivated; but items which rank low for the non-motivated scatter all along the scale for the motivated. This suggests that we have three types of items here:

    1) Items which are high on effectiveness for both motivated and non-motivated.

---

[1] Cf. Table 17 in Chapter I of this Part, for the numbering and definition of the effects.

2) Items which are high for the motivated but not high for the non-motivated.

3) Items which are relatively low for both motivated and non-motivated.

The first group can be thought of as the *strong effects,* since they rank high for both groups. We can also infer that the program has something to do with them, since they turn up relatively frequently among the non-motivated, who are under no psychological pressure to report the effects. The second group can be thought of as *"motivationally contingent"* since they are only frequent among those who came into the program with these aims in mind. These may still be thought of as true effects, though, since there is another group of effects which ranks lower. The third group, *weak effects,* consists of those items which rank relatively low among both those who were motivated and non-motivated.

The vertical and horizontal lines in tables 29, 30 and 31 were drawn in an informal way to divide the effects according to our definitions.

Although individual exceptions do appear, the general pattern of the correlation is similar in all three tables. This, in itself, is worth noting, as it suggests that, unlike motivation, the effect of exposure is additive. That is, in a way, additional years of exposure increase the probability of each effect to about the same extent. This means that our data do not suggest that there are "early," "middle," and "late" effects, but rather that the longer a person has been in the program the more likely he is to report any effect.

Out of the total of 23 effects, 15 were classified the same way in each of the three exposure groups, and eight were classified the same in two and differently in the third. No effect was classified a different way in each year.

Tables 29, 30 and 31 appear on following page.

We can now make a tabular summary of the reported effects:

I. *Relatively Strong Effects*

    1. Great minds . . .

    3. Analyze and criticize . . .

    5. Talking with more intellectual people . . .

    6. Improving my reading skills.

    7. Express ideas . . .

  10. Making new friends.

  11. Gaining insight into myself.

  18. Meeting people who are quite different.

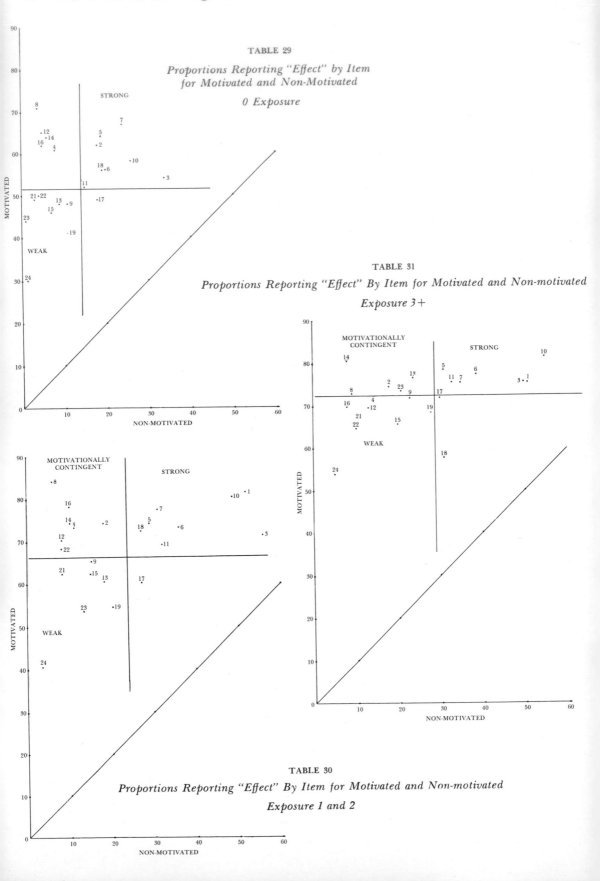

TABLE 29

*Proportions Reporting "Effect" by Item
for Motivated and Non-Motivated*

0 Exposure

TABLE 31

Proportions Reporting "Effect" By Item for Motivated and Non-motivated

Exposure 3+

TABLE 30

Proportions Reporting "Effect" By Item for Motivated and Non-motivated

Exposure 1 and 2

II. *Motivationally Contingent Effects*
    2. Reacquainting myself . . .
    4. Escaping . . . occupation.
    8. Escaping . . . housewife.
   12. Escaping . . . community.
   14. Supplementing narrow college . . .
   16. Developing common interests with my spouse.

III. *Relatively Weak Effects*
    9. Improving my taste in fiction and poetry.
   13. Becoming sure of myself . . .
   15. Gaining a better intellectual background for participation in community affairs.
   19. Finding solutions to contemporary problems.
   21. Improving my ability to carry out my job through the intellectual training of reading Great Books.
   22. Increasing . . . job ability . . . through group discussion.
   23. Developing ability to lead discussions outside of Great Books.
   24. Gaining the equivalent of a college education.

IV. *Unclassifiable*
   17. Becoming a more effective participant in group discussions outside of Great Books.

Classifications I through III can be thought of as a very rough ordering of effects of the program from those which are frequent effects in both the motivated and non-motivated, through those which are frequent only among the motivated, to those which are infrequent in both motivated and non-motivated participants. Motive 17 is a continual puzzle, each time falling in a logically puzzling category of being *relatively* higher for non-motivated than motivated. Perhaps becoming a good group participant is like finding the bluebird of happiness, a goal which cannot be directly pursued.

The ordering of the effects in terms of their relative potency raises the question as to whether we can find some underlying factors which may account for the differences. There are some clues in the data.

The number of instances being small, our conclusions must be tentative, but it does appear that the modal or most common motives have a higher batting average than the less frequent motives. This, of course, augurs well for the program, as it suggests that it can deliver (at least in terms of subjective impressions) precisely what its clientele most wants. Is this because, say, the "process" is essentially social and a group needs a certain proportion of people wanting something before that something turns up, or is it because the frequent motives are different in character from the infrequent ones? The former hypothesis is intriguing but we have not had the opportunity to explore it. There is some evidence, however, to support the second idea. Let us begin by examining the relative effectiveness of the motives when they are classified by the "clusters" described in the preceding chapter.

TABLE 32

Cluster and Effectiveness

Cluster	More Effective	Less Effective
"Cosmopolitanism"	3	0
"Content"	2	2
"Self-Help"	1	3
"Stepping Stone"	0	3

Although the numbers are *very* small, and we must be cautious in our interpretation, it does look as if "Content" makes some difference. All three items in "Cosmopolitanism" are among the relatively more effective, and three of the items in "Stepping Stone" are among the relatively ineffective — a fourth item in "Stepping Stone" is our unclassifiable friend — "Becoming a more effective participant in group discussions outside of Great Books."

As a final attempt at looking for some pattern, let us classify these effects into three groups: 1) those effects which are completely personal, in the sense of involving only the Great Books and the reader (e.g., "To learn what the greatest minds have to say"); 2) those effects which involve the person and the discussion group, but no one else (e.g., "Meeting people who are quite different from me"); and 3) those effects whose existence depends not only on the participant and/or the group, but also on some sort of involvement with the world outside of the program. Table 33 gives the relative effectiveness for these three types.

TABLE 33

*Type of Effect and Effectiveness**

Effectiveness	Personal	Group	Extra-Program	Unclassifiable
Relatively high ...	4 (1, 3, 6, 11)	4 (5, 7, 10, 18)		
Motivationally contingent	5 (2, 14, 8, 4, 12)			1 (16)**
Relatively low	2 (9, 24)		6 (13, 15, 19, 21, 22, 23)	

* The numbers in the parentheses are the specific motivations; the numbers to the left are the total number in the cell.

** This motivation ("developing common interests with my spouse") couldn't be classified as its status would depend on whether the spouse attended the discussion group, something which we know varies a lot.

Table 33 suggests the following: first of all, all of the effects which require the involvement of the participant in something, or with somebody, outside of the program, are relatively low on effectiveness. Whether the arena is the job, community affairs, sociability, or the solution of contemporary problems, all of these effects are in the low group. Conversely, all of the effects which involve the person and the immediate discussion group are at the top of the heap, for both motivated and non-motivated people. We can see this contrast by comparing two somewhat similar items, "Getting a chance to express ideas I had been thinking and reading about" (7) and "Developing the ability to lead discussions outside of Great Books" (23).

TABLE 34

Effectiveness of Items 7 and 23

Per cent reporting the effect

Exposure (years)	Motivated		Non-Motivated	
	Express Ideas	Lead Outside	Express Ideas	Lead Outside
0	67 (237)	44 (75)	24 (506)	1 (668)
1 & 2	77 (175)	53 (36)	31 (398)	13 (537)
3 or more	76 (111)	74 (38)	35 (340)	21 (413)
	(Base N in parentheses)			

The contrast is consistent. While Table 34 shows our standard effects of motivation and exposure on effectiveness, it also shows, in each case, higher effectiveness for "expressing ideas" than for leading outside. Now, the two activities are probably fairly similar in their nature, but the one can be "consummated" immediately in the program, while the other requires getting involved in the world outside of the self and the program.

The purely "personal" things lie between these two, most having high effectiveness, but two ("Improving my taste in fiction and poetry" and "Gaining the equivalent of a college education") are both in the low area. Why they should differ we don't know, really, except that our chapter on poetry does little to suggest that false modesty accounts for the finding. Rather, as the supporters of the program would be the first to acknowledge, we might attribute it to the fact that purely esthetic matters are given little emphasis in the readings. Maybe the best way to explain the college one (a very rare motive, reported by only seven per cent of the respondents) is to say that it is clearly impossible to gain the equivalent of a college education from Great Books, and no one really claims that it should be possible. These people, in effect, are looking for the wrong thing.

Now, it is about time to re-stress that our classification is relative. There is no subgroup in which there is 100 per cent effectiveness for our "high items" and no group with zero effectiveness for the low items. In fact, reference to Table 34 will show that in the advanced years, for the motivated, 74 per cent report high effectiveness for leading groups outside.

If we think of the advanced-year, motivated group, as the most "sensitized" we find no single effect with less than half reporting positive results, regardless of the relative standing on the scale. To put this, itself, in further perspective, among the advanced-year, non-motivated — people who liked the program well enough to stay in it, but didn't come seeking the specific effects — we find more than 50 per cent reporting effectiveness for only two things: "Learning what the great minds have to say" (54 per cent), and "Making new friends" (55 per cent). Instead of a crutch, relativity thus appears to be a two-edged sword. Among the motivated, a relatively less effective item still has a very high percentage, but among the non-motivated, a relatively highly effective item tends to have a rather low absolute percentage.

We began with the question of whether we should think of the program as essentially a projective thing in which you got what you wanted (or maybe wanted what you got) or whether there were definite areas in which the nature of the program was a determinant regardless of motives. The answer is apparently that motivation is not the entire story. There are some effects which are reported relatively frequently among both motivated and non-motivated; some effects which are reported relatively infrequently by both; as well as a number which appear to be definitely "contingent on motivation."

Summary

While "testimonial" evidence must be regarded with dread and foreboding by the "scientific" researcher, we felt that we would not be severing ourselves from respectability if we asked what the participants thought they got out of the program. We began with the general question of "impact," and saw that there were strong impact differences. Perceptions of impact: a) increase with exposure, either because of true changes or because of drop-outs, or both; b) decrease with education and age, controlling for education; c) increase with the total number of motives reported.

When, subsequently, we turned to an analysis of specific motives, we found that they, too, varied with exposure and motivation, but through some statistical maneuvers we managed to arrive at the conclusion that motivation does not explain the whole thing. Rather, there appear to be three types of effects: a) relatively high effects which are reported frequently by both motivated and non-motivated; b) motivationally contingent effects, which are frequently reported only by the people who are motivated to seek them (the number of men reporting that they have escaped the intellectual narrowness of being a housewife is quite small); and c) relatively low effects which are less often reported by both motivated and non-motivated. The major differences between the stronger and weaker effects may be interpreted as reflecting the difference between aims which may be reached within the program itself and aims which require a plunge into the frigid waters of the natural environment before the shore is reached.

Can any of our analysis answer the question, "Is the program effective?" We doubt it if the question is meant in the sense of giving Great Books an A, B, C, D, or F, in "effectiveness." However, we would like to suggest the following generalizations which follow from the analysis of this chapter.

First, despite our worry about drop-out rates, we think that any informal organization which meets twice a month to talk about books must be considered seriously if from 20 to 70 per cent (depending on the exposure and educational group) say "It has had a genuine impact on me," when the speakers are drawn from the most highly educated strata of the country and are heavily involved in other community and civic affairs.

Second, we believe that Great Books must be considered from a special point of view, given our findings on motivation. Most adult programs of an "educational" nature have very specific aims, whether they are changing attitudes toward minority groups, teaching proficiency on the recorder, getting people ready for jobs as hotel managers, or instruction in automobile repairing. In contrast, Great Books should probably be thought of as a catalyst whose essential function is to speed up or facilitate a sort of "chemical" process involving the individual, the books, the group, and the real world in which the meaning of the books is to be acted on. If the reaction is sometimes slow, or the energy produced minimal, it is hard to say that this is because of the program. Thus, while it is true that "finding solutions to contemporary problems" is not one of the program's strongest points, at least part of the situation may be due to the fact that the program may not recruit people who are highly motivated to find these solutions in the readings (only 15 per cent of the sample checked this as a motive), and another goodly part is probably due to the fact that in contemporary society the probability that any one individual can do much about any particular "social problem" is low.[2]

Finally, we should note that another way of reading the results on effectiveness is that while concrete changes in the "outside world" are relatively low on the effectiveness thermometer, those things which are high have a gratifyingly "intellectual" tinge. While the professional sociologist expects that any group which meets regularly over a period of years will,

---

[2] The reader who is seriously interested in "evaluating" Great Books should read, in addition to this report, Philip Jacob's *Changing Values in College,* an evaluation of the effectiveness of American universities which draws particularly disenchanted conclusions. Cf., Philip E. Jacob, *Changing Values in College, An Exploratory Study of the Impact of College Teaching,* New York, Harper & Brothers, 1957.

nay *must*, develop a high degree of "social" and "sociable" elements, the high-ranking effects are not of the "kaffee-klatsch" type, but include such cerebral things as learning what the great minds have to say, analyzing and criticizing arguments, expressing ideas, and gaining self-insight. Those motivations (other than "Cosmopolitanism," which, as we have noted, has a heavy intellectual component) which smack of social climbing, or patina polishing ("Self-Help"), or the strictly gimmick-oriented stripe ("Stepping Stone"), are much less frequently reported as high on effectiveness. While some of the later chapters may, in truth, be read to suggest that many of the intellectual changes are not overwhelming in strength and frequency, nothing in our data on motivations and perception of effects suggests that the basic idea of the program — reading and discussion of Great Books — takes a subsidiary role in any important number of groups.

Part C
STATISTICAL
ASSESSMENTS

STATISTICAL ASSESSMENTS

Introduction

While no survey research worker wishes even to entertain the notion that his respondents are not being candid, one may still wish for "harder" evidence on the effects of Great Books than the respondents' own testimonials. In the remaining chapters of this report we shall discuss our indirect measures of effect — test items, reports on behavior, and indirect questions — all of which attempt to gain a more objective picture of changes in the participants' intellectual skills, attitudes, and behavior which follow from their exposure to Great Books.

We are, alas, forced to begin with a methodological discussion. Since it is extremely important, we will attempt to outline it quickly so that the reader may proceed to the detailed findings.

To begin with, the only scientifically valid method of measuring the effectiveness of Great Books is to take a large number of people and (1) assign a random proportion to Great Books, (2) make sure that the remainder are insulated from Great Books, and (3) measure both groups repeatedly over a period of time. If the results show that the Great Books group change more than the "controls," we may assume that Great Books has an effect. Now, such an experiment was both impossible and unrealistic. It was impossible because our study had to be completed in one year. It was unrealistic because there is no way to insulate adult controls from influences similar to Great Books. Hence, even a realistic experiment would have to include other programs such as college extension work, personal reading programs, informal discussion groups, etc., in order to ask the question, "Given that Great Books might make a difference, does it make more of a difference than other educational stimuli?"

What we did instead was to compare the statistical scores of beginning and advanced group members, dividing the participants into three groups: (a) those who had completed less than one year, (b) those who had completed one or two years, and (c) those who had completed three or more years, in Great Books. This measure was calculated for each respondent, regardless of his year of reading. Thus, new members to the program, even in ninth-year groups, were scored as zero on years of exposure.

If the program does have effects, then advanced-year participants should show different statistical scores from those of beginners. Is the converse true? Unfortunately not, for we might get a spurious difference if:

a) Persons who drop out of the program are selected on the variable in question. For instance, if Democrats have a higher drop-out rate than Republicans (they don't, by the way), then advanced-year groups should have a greater proportion of Republicans, and we would draw the false conclusion that Great Books makes people more Republican.

b) Everybody tends to change in a given direction as he grows older. Thus, if everybody joined Great Books at the age of 35, we would find that third-year people had an average age of 37 and falsely conclude that Great Books ages people.

c) The program is now recruiting people who differ from previous recruits. Thus, if in recent years Great Books tended to recruit more and more Democrats proportionally, we would find more Republicans in advanced-year groups and again draw a false conclusion about political changes.

A statistician can deduce a number of other horrifying possibilities, but these will do for the moment.

As a matter of fact, we shall ignore threats "b" and "c" in our analyses, mostly because there is nothing much we can do about them. In terms of "c," however, we can state that comparison with previous surveys of Great Books within the last decade indicates little or no difference between our sample and earlier samples in terms of age, sex, education, etc., and any historical shifts are probably of a fairly subtle nature.

The drop-out problem is, however, a serious one, as we have seen that, unlike the army, the prison, and other more favored educational institutions, Great Books has little control over its dissatisfied members. In our original report we attempted to grapple with this problem through a long series of statistical tests and comparisons, which, while self-admittedly ingenious, were at best suggestive. Recently, however, an opportunity arose for making a better check. The sponsors of this study, in the fall of 1958, granted funds for a brief follow-up of our sample groups. We didn't re-interview our respondents, but we did go back to the group leaders and attempt to find out whether the participants in our study were still in Great Books. In a little over ninety per cent of the cases, we were successful. Thus, for almost all of our respondents we can classify them as "Continued" or "Dropped-out" in 1958. Since we are not here concerned with analysis of the dynamics of program retention, our classification ignores reasons for dropping out (although we have data on them) and the question of whether the continuation was with the same group.

The following table will illustrate how we can use these data as a control for spurious effects due to program attrition.

TABLE 35

Drop-Out Control for "Making New Friends"
Per cent reporting "Making new friends" as an effect

1957 Exposure (years)	1958 Status		
	Dropped	Continued	Total
3+	51 (94)	64 (330)	61 (424)
1 and 2	56 (135)	60 (404)	58 (539)
0	32 (298)	39 (346)	36 (644)
	(Base N in parentheses)		

What do we make out of Table 35? If we look in the right-hand column, we find what would turn up in a cross-sectional comparison of participants grouped on exposure. Since the per cent reporting "Making new friends" as an effect increases with exposure, we would conclude that one of the effects of Great Books is just that.

When we compare the Dropped and Continued, however, we find in each case that the drop-outs were a little less likely to report having made new friends. Therefore, our drop-out specter looms. Let us, however, consider the comparisons marked with arrows in Table 35. If we compare the 0-exposure "Continued" with the 1-and-2-exposure "Total" (both measured in the fall of 1957), we find a comparison which is relatively purified of drop-outs. (We say "relatively" because the 2's are not controlled for the persons who dropped out after the first year.) Hence, we will assume that *the people in a given year who did not drop out are essentially like the total group in the next higher exposure category, except that the latter have been in Great Books longer.* In our example we find a difference in each of the "arrow" comparisons, and hence we conclude that people do make friends (mostly in the first year) in Great Books, even though those who do not make friends tend disproportionately to drop out.

Because, however, these data were not available to us when we wrote our original report, the following sections are not merely a condensation of the report but, to some extent, a re-analysis. Luckily, however, in most instances our original conjectures from manipulation of the cross-sectional data were borne out when the drop-out control was applied.

We shall now consider a number of particular effects, along with a few non-effects. Following the theme suggested in our analysis of self-assessments, we shall group the effects in terms of a gradient from personal to extra-program. Chapter 1 concerns such purely intra-personal effects as knowledge, esthetic taste, and reading habits. Chapter 2 treats personal value changes, ideological effects, and community involvement.

CHAPTER ONE

KNOWLEDGE, ESTHETICS, AND READING

In this chapter we shall consider the effects of Great Books in three different intellectual areas: knowledge of the traditional liberal arts, esthetic taste in classical music and in poetry, and patterns of reading. These three are grouped together since they share the common properties of being "intellectual" and do not necessarily involve the participant in any sort of personal or social "action." Considered together, the three analyses give us a rough sort of profile of the purely "intellectual" effects of the program.

Knowledge

In this section we shall examine in some detail the "knowledge" of the participants, not in the sense of their general store of facts about the batting averages of Babe Ruth or the members of the cabinet of President Buchanan, but rather in the sense of their familiarity with that part of the general culture which can be called "the liberal arts and humanities"; their store of information about Martin Luther, Mozart, Aristophanes, the French Revolution, Galileo, etc.

In the totality of potential effects, it is clear that sheer accumulation of knowledge is not one of the major aims of Great Books. Rather, the program is aimed at promoting more subtle qualities, such as critical thinking, ability to analyze and evaluate readings, and increased intellectual sophistication. Thus, evidence that an increase in knowledge exists is not *ipso facto* evidence that the program is succeeding in all of its aims. Nevertheless, the *failure* of several years of exposure to Great Books to yield any increase in knowledge of the humanities would, in itself, probably be sufficient to cast doubt on any hypotheses about more sophisticated effects. In short, if the important effects of the program are presumed to follow from increased acquaintance with the humanities, it is necessary to begin by asking whether such an increase actually occurs.

The Picture Test

The basic measure used in our study is the identification test, a copy of which is included here. It is a somewhat unorthodox instrument of measurement and requires preliminary discussion before we proceed to present our data. (For brevity, in tabular data hereafter we shall refer to this identification test with the phrase "Test Score.")

The test consists of thirty-two cartoons which originally appeared in *Life* magazine in 1950.[1] The pictures were developed and drawn by Charles E. Martin, a professional artist.[2] According to the *Life* text, they were developed to reflect the famous "core curriculum" of Columbia University. As far as Mr. Martin and we know, they have never been used for research purposes. Nevertheless, they appealed to us as a possible measure in our study for the following two reasons: a) to a striking extent, they cover the curriculum of Great Books, twenty of the thirty-one directly referring to specific Great Books readings, and many of the remainder referring to authors and ideas which are presumably frequently mentioned in the discussions; b) the whimsical quality of the cartoons appeared to us to be a good way to motivate the cooperation of volunteer respondents who might well be threatened or bored by an "outright" test. Our impression is that we were quite correct on the latter assumption, for our field interviewers reported that most groups were quite taken with the cartoons, and we received a number of requests for answers from the Great Books participants who took part in the study.

---

[1] *Life*, Vol. 29, No. 16 (October 16, 1950), 23-33.

[2] Mr. Martin, who holds the copyright to the pictures, very kindly gave us permission to use them in our research.

Each of the 32 drawings on this and the following pages should suggest something—some book, person, episode, or work of art. Please jot down next to each picture a word or phrase which identifies it. Guess if you are not certain. (The first answer has been given as an example.)

"Sir Walter Raleigh

spreading his cape

for Queen Elizabeth"

HISTORY AND POLITICS

LITERATURE

Answers to Picture Test

1. Sir Walter Raleigh spreading his cape for Queen Elizabeth.
2. King John signing Magna Carta.
3. Tennis-court Oath, French Revolution.
4. Martin Luther and his ninety-five theses.
5. British suffragettes who chained themselves to the fence outside the Houses of Parliament.
6. Machiavelli, *The Prince*. (Prince should be a combination of the Lion and the Fox.)
7. Jean Marat, assassinated by Charlotte Corday during the French Revolution.
8. Rousseau's idea of the noble savage.
9. Darwin's theory of evolution.
10. Karl Marx and his theory of Capitalism.
11. Galileo testing his law of falling bodies at the Tower of Pisa.
12. Isaac Newton and his law of gravity.
13. Freud, *Psychoanalysis*.
14. Saint Augustine stealing a pear. (Related in the *Confessions*.)
15. Nietzsche, theory of the Superman in *Also Sprach Zarathustra*.
16. Malthus and his theory of eventual overpopulation of the earth.
17. John Locke.
18. Job.
19. Aristophanes, *The Clouds, The Birds, The Frogs*.
20. Dante, *The Inferno*.
21. Shelley, *Prometheus Unbound*.
22. Rabelais, *Gargantua & Pantagruel*.
23. Milton, the fallen angels in *Paradise Lost*.
24. Shakespeare, Birnam Wood coming to Dunsinane, in *Macbeth*.
25. Swift, Houyhnhnms in *Gulliver's Travels*.
26. Cervantes, *Don Quixote*.
27. Voltaire, "Cultivate your own garden," in *Candide*.
28. Wagner, *Ring of the Nibelungen*.
29. Michelangelo painting the ceiling of the Sistine Chapel.
30. Mozart.
31. Beethoven destroying dedication of the *Third Symphony (Eroica)* to Napoleon.
32. Renoir, who had the brush tied to his hand when arthritis deprived him of the free use of his hands.

Since, however, in research, whimsical is as whimsical does, it is necessary to consider some of the technical problems of the measurement quality of the instrument. The first question is that of the "validity" of the test, i.e., what the test measures. Our working assumption is that the cartoon test measures the individual's familiarity with certain "high points" of Western "high" culture. It does not, we must stress, probe into the finer questions of analytical acumen or depth of knowledge. Thus, while we do not have to believe that everyone who said "Don Quixote" to Cartoon No. 26 is an expert on Spanish literature and culture, it is fairly reasonable to infer that the respondent who said "Hans Brinker" is not.[3] In short, we have little to offer but "face validity"; however, the pattern of correlations reported later in this memorandum (e.g., relations to formal education and to musical taste, and data from the Northwestern University sample) in no way challenges our assumptions about the qualities measured by the test. To sum up, both face validity and the pattern of correlates argue that our test is in some very general way a measure of knowledge in the area of humanities. The exact "depth" of this knowledge is, however, unknown.

As is traditional in sociological research, the paucity of our data on validity is partially offset by a fairly good set of data on internal consistency. Each answer to the test was scored simply as correct or incorrect, excluding any gradations of rightness or wrongness.[4] Although this undoubtedly resulted in scoring as "wrong" a number of subjects whose answers were not far off, our assumption was that the net effect of these decisions would be merely that of raising or lowering the "cutting-point" of a given item.

The question of internal consistency is essentially that of asking if, regardless of whether the exact name (validity) of the dimension measured is known, it is reasonable to treat the data as measuring a single dimension or whether we must assume that several measurement dimensions are involved. We have treated the cartoons as measures of a single dimension for the following reasons:

1) *Item intercorrelations.* To the extent that each of the cartoons tends to measure the same dimension of content, it should show a strong statistical association with every other cartoon in the set. We did not compute each of the 435 possible intercorrelations,[5] but rather drew a probability sample of possible interrelations, stratified in such a way that each cartoon appeared once and only once in the set of fifteen. For each, "Q" (a measure of association for "qualitative" data which is analogous to a correlation

---

[3] When, of course, you come to the respondent who answered "Maria Callas" for the Wagnerian dragon in Cartoon 28, the issue is somewhat less clear, but fortunately only a handful of respondents took the task as a challenge to their wit instead of their memory. We were forced to exclude only one out of 1909 cartoon quizzes on the grounds of unmitigated frivolousness.

[4] Josef Zelan of NORC had the task of making these 57,270 decisions, and his monotonous but vital contribution to the study is hereby acknowledged.

[5] There are 32 cartoons in the set. Cartoon 1 was answered in the printed protocol as an example, and Cartoon 5 (the British suffragette) was arbitrarily excluded from the scoring on the basis of difficulties in achieving reliable coding. The remaining 30 cartoons have a possible 435 intercorrelations.

coefficient for numerical data) was computed. We found all of the inter-correlations to be positive, with a median value of .54.

2) *Sub-section Correlations.* The cartoons were grouped by Mr. Martin into the following: (a) History and Politics, (b) Science and Philosophy, (c) Literature, and (d) Music and Art. If the test actually includes several dimensions of content, we would expect this to be reflected in the inter-correlations of these sections. To test this hypothesis, each sub-section was dichotomized at its median number of correct answers, and Q's were computed. The results are presented in Table 36.

TABLE 36

Q Associations Among Sub-Sections of the Picture Test

	Science and Philosophy	Literature	Music and Art
History and Politics	.69	.72	.58
Science and Philosophy		.80	.71
Literature			.70

The associations are fairly high, and there is no indication that any one section has a pattern which would suggest that it taps a separate dimension.

3) *Northwestern Sample.* In order to get some data for comparison with our sample, we arranged to collect a small number of protocols from undergraduate students at Northwestern University.[6] The test was administered to all the members of two classes, a freshman course in composition and literature, and an advanced course in American literature for upperclassmen, 97 cases in all. The sample is, of course, not a probability sample of the Northwestern student body. We felt, however, that similar data from a group of undergraduates at a high-ranking university would give us some comparisons with our Great Books sample. In terms of internal consistency, it appears that the Northwestern sample gives back results which are essentially similar to our survey data. For the same fifteen sampled item intercorrelations we got a median Q of .51. We compared the rank order of the marginals for the thirty cartoons in the samples and found a rank correlation of .84, which suggests that the same cartoons tended to be "easy" or "difficult" in the two groups. In short, there is nothing in this comparison to indicate that the internal consistency reported for our survey is spurious.

In summary, a number of rule-of-thumb procedures suggest that we would be in no serious danger if we treated the entire batch of cartoons as a measure of a single dimension of information about liberal arts and humanities.

---

[6] Morris Sunshine, graduate student in sociology at Northwestern, administered the questionnaires for us.

Quiz Scores and Exposure

Let us begin by asking whether there is a relationship between years of exposure to Great Books and scores on the test.

TABLE 37

Years of Exposure and Test Scores

	Years of Great Books Completed		
	0	1 and 2	3 or more
Per cent with 11 or more correct	39	48	67
N	(723)	(553)	(434)

For the comparison between 0 and 1 and 2, $x^2 = 9.417$, $p < .01$

For the comparison between 1 and 2 and 3 or more, $x^2 = 35.182$, $p < .001$

Clearly there is a relationship. The per cent getting eleven or more correct increases from a little more than one-third in the first year to two-thirds in the group which has completed three or more years, and the differences are highly reliable statistically.

Since there are no important educational differences in the exposure groups, the test-score differences cannot be a function of educational composition. Nevertheless, let us look at education and exposure simultaneously to see what the pattern is.

TABLE 38

Education, Exposure, and Test Scores

Per cent scoring 11 or more

Participant's Education	Years of Great Books Completed		
	0	1 and 2	3 or more
No college	11 (116)	36 (75)	47 (73)
Part college	29 (161)	42 (123)	72 (93)
Bachelor's degree	50 (163)	52 (136)	66 (84)
Graduate study	55 (246)	64 (210)	76 (169)

(Base N in parentheses)

Table 38 indicates, as we would expect, that scores vary with both exposure and with education. That is, within each exposure group, the scores increase with education, and within each educational group the scores increase with exposure. At one extreme we find the non-college first-year participants, with 11 per cent above the median on the test; and at the opposite extreme, the advanced-year participants with graduate work, 76 per cent of whom are above the median.

It is perhaps worth noting, also, that there appears to be an "interaction" in the table in that the educational differences vary in "strength" with years of exposure. In the first year the graduate group has five times as many high scorers as the non-college, and almost twice as many as the part-college. In the most advanced group, however, the graduate-work group has less than twice as many high scores as the non-college, and the differences within the college group are negligible. In short, *with additional years of exposure to Great Books, educational differences bulk smaller and smaller in cartoon scores.* The less-educated participant appears considerably disadvantaged at the beginning of his participation but less so as time goes on. In the advanced years, exposure to Great Books seems to have cancelled out educational differences other than college vs. non-college.

Another perspective on the relationship between education and scores on our test is given by the Northwestern University data. Despite the small number of cases and admitted sample bias, they can give us some hints as to how our entering Great Books participants would compare with contemporary undergraduates. Table 39 gives the results.

TABLE 39

Year in College and Test Scores in Northwestern Sample

	Year in College	
	Freshman	Junior and Senior
Per cent scoring 11 or more	11	45
N	(37)	(51)

By the definitions used in our survey sample, all of the Northwestern students would have been scored as "part college," but it may be of some utility to divide them roughly between the 37 freshmen who were only in their second quarter of college and the 51 juniors and seniors who were near the end of their undergraduate studies. When we compare these groups with the Great Books sample, we find that the freshmen score considerably like the "non-college" Great Books participants, while the upper-classmen approximate the "bachelor's-degree" level for entering participants. Our Great Books beginners seem to score neither conspicuously higher nor conspicuously lower than the contemporary undergraduates. If, however, we take into consideration that Northwestern is a high-ranking university, and our Great Books participants enter the program usually more than a decade past their undergraduate training, our guess would be that even on entry, Great Books people score somewhat higher than their formal level of training would indicate. Likewise, we may hazard the *guess* that the advanced-year Great Books participant, regardless of level of formal education, compares rather favorably in his scores with persons still in the process of studying the liberal arts. This latter conclusion is reinforced when we note that the upper-classmen in the N.U. sample were drawn from an advanced English course, which probably attracts students especially interested in the humanities.

Now let us see whether application of our control for drop-outs would lead us to modify our conclusions.

TABLE 40

Drop-Out Control for Test

Per cent scoring 11 or more correct

1957 Exposure (years)	1958 Status		
	Dropped	Continued	Total
3+	61 (89)	69 (319)	67 (408)
1 and 2	50 (125)	53 (396)	52 (521)
0	37 (287)	42 (340)	40 (627)

(Base N in parentheses)

There is a statistically significant tendency for low scorers to drop out of the program (p.<.01), but our two control comparisons are each in the expected direction, and each is statistically significant at a probability of .01 or less. Therefore, although the cross-sectional data overestimate the strength of the relationship, we have grounds to believe that exposure to Great Books leads to considerable increase in familiarity with the liberal arts.

Esthetics

While we should have been rather disappointed if we had found no gain in knowledge of the liberal arts, our assessment of changes in esthetic preference and sensitivity should be viewed from a slightly different perspective. Although a large number of the readings in the program may be classified as "art," inspection of the curriculum suggests that esthetic matters are given less stress than philosophic, theological, and political issues. Nevertheless, a consideration of possible gains in the area of poetic taste and musical sophistication may be worth our time for two reasons: first, any fair evaluation of a program should not only examine what that program does, but also attempt to find what it does not do. Negative findings in these unstressed areas would lead us to believe that Great Books is not an educational cure-all, but that it has certain areas of strong effect and other areas of lesser effect. Second, one of the beliefs of the proponents of the program is that adult liberal education has a proliferating effect and spreads beyond the immediate subject matter. Thus, even though we would not expect to find that esthetic differences were as strong as knowledge differences, a slight increase in esthetic skills would tend to support the claim that Great Books has a generalized influence on the participants' intellectual lives.

Therefore, let us consider the data collected on two measures, one of musical sophistication, and one of ability to judge poetry.

Music

Our measure of musical sophistication was developed as follows: In our questionnaire we listed thirteen "classical" musical compositions. They were selected arbitrarily on the assumption that they covered a range of musical sophistication ranging from the "lower-middlebrow" (*The 1812 Overture, Nutcracker Suite, William Tell Overture*) through the "upper-middlebrow" (Brahms' *Second Piano Concerto*, Beethoven's *Seventh Symphony*, Brahms' *First Symphony*) to the "highbrow" (*Missa Papae Marcelli*, by Palestrina, Ives' *Second Symphony*, Beethoven's *Variations on a Theme by Diabelli*).

The respondents were given the following instructions:
"Let's assume that you are going to a concert tomorrow, and the following musical works might be on the program. Rate each in terms of its familiarity, as follows:

"1) Very familiar — I'd recognize it if I heard it, even if the title wasn't announced.

"2) Familiar — I might not know the title just from hearing it played, but it's something I've heard before and know a little about.

"3) Less familiar — I don't know much about this specific work, but I am relatively familiar with the composer and the general type of music he is known for.

"4) Unfamiliar — as far as I know, I've never heard of this work, and I know little or nothing about the composer."

Those who survived reading these lengthy instructions then proceeded to check the thirteen musical titles.

Inspection of the data from our survey sample indicated that the effective range we could hope to get was between the non-musical and the upper-middlebrow, since very few respondents checked the highbrow titles as familiar (only 45 out of 1,909 checked the Diabelli variations as "very familiar," and only 72 checked the Ives symphony as "very familiar" or "familiar").

From the titles with less extreme frequencies, we selected four as the possible components of a (no pun intended) musical scale. They were: *The 1812 Overture* (80 per cent "very familiar" or "familiar"), Brahms' *First Symphony* (59 per cent "very familiar" or "familiar"), Mozart's "*Jupiter*" *Symphony* (43 per cent "very familiar" or "familiar"), and Beethoven's "*Archduke*" *Trio* (20 per cent "very familiar" or "familiar").

Table 41 indicates that these four items will make an excellent Guttman-type scale. A Guttman scale (named after its author) is a pattern of responses to a set of items which indicates that the items may be considered as measuring a single dimension of content. In practice, formal statistical criteria are used, but the general idea is a simple one. If the dimension is scalable, the pattern of responses (as in Scale Types I-IV in Table 41) should form a step pattern, so that a person who has a plus on a given hard item (say, the "Jupiter" Symphony) always has a plus on the easier items. The more people who fit into the step pattern, the more confidence we have in the scalability of the dimension — i.e., confidence that our music items tap the same thing.

TABLE 41a

Musical Sophistication — Scalability

		Item			
1812	Brahms	Jupiter	Archduke	Scale Type	N
+	+	+	+	I	258
+	+	+	−	II	350
+	+	−	−	III	277
+	−	−	−	IV	327
−	−	−	−	V	242
		Error Types			
+	−	+	−		77
−	+	−	−		53
+	+	−	+		26
−	+	+	+		21
+	−	+	+		19
+	+	+	+		12
−	−	+	−		9
−	+	+	−		8
−	−	+	+		3
−	−	+	+		1
−	+	+	+		0
					1,693

Reproducibility = .963

TABLE 41b

Musical Sophistication — Item Inter-Association (Q)

	Brahms	Jupiter	Archduke
1812	.702	.784	.623
Brahms		.827	.780
Jupiter			.813

Both the reproducibility coefficient and the item inter-associations suggest that our index is highly consistent internally and will make a respectable cumulative scale in the sense that a person who claims familiarity with the *"Archduke" Trio* has a high probability of also claiming familiarity with the three other items; a person who claims familiarity with the *"Jupiter"* also will tend to claim familiarity with the *1812* and Brahms, etc.

It should be noted, however, that we have no way of telling the degree to which the subjects have "inflated" or "deflated" their true levels of knowledge. There was nothing in the measure to prohibit a less knowledgeable person from claiming a high level of musical sophistication. Nevertheless, we may assume that "inflation" is not rampant, for if there were wholesale "guessing," we should not get the internal consistency we have observed. Thus, if the respondents are "cheating," they are apparently cheating in a non-random fashion, which, in this situation, by definition, is not cheating.

Let us now see whether musical knowledge increases in the same fashion as knowledge of answers to our quiz.

TABLE 42

Exposure and Musical Sophistication, Controlling for Drop-Out

Per cent high on music scale*

1957 Exposure (years)	1958 Status		
	Dropped	Total	Continued
3+	38 (74)	46 (299)	45 (373)
1 and 2	48 (122)	36 (377)	39 (499)
0	33 (267)	43 (304)	38 (571)

(Base N in parentheses)

* High score=Scale Types I and II in Table 41a and those ambiguous responses assigned to Types I and II by the writers.

While the cross-sectional comparisons in the Total column suggest a slight increase with exposure, the over-all pattern is inconsistent, and the over-all differences are not statistically significant. Thus, we may conclude that the demonstrated increase in liberal arts knowledge does not generalize to increased acquaintance with classical music. While the musical interests of the participants are undoubtedly more sophisticated than those of the general public, they have their roots outside the program.

Poetry

Although there is little or no "lyric poetry" in the Great Books readings, the participant who continues in the program eventually will have read a considerable amount of verse. Even before he gets to the fourth year when Aristotle's *Poetics* presumably tell him what to make of it, he will have read a large amount of verse drama (Shakespeare, Aeschylus, Sophocles) and epic poetry (Homer). In the fourth and later years he will add Milton, Dante, *The Song of the Volsungs and the Nibelungs* and more Shakespeare and Aeschylus. While heavy doses of Calvin's *Institutes* and St. Thomas may offset these, the fact remains that Great Books participants have been exposed to quite a bit of poetry.

It is suggested, therefore, that one of the effects of participation in the program may be increased sensitivity to excellence in verse. Remembering back to Chapter I of Part 8, we note that 24 per cent of the sample checked "Improving my taste in fiction and poetry" as a reason for joining. Now Chapter II of Part B indicated that this motive belongs in the "less successful" pile, but just as we don't take the respondent's word for the successes, we want to make a more sophisticated check before we conclude that the program does not increase these abilities.

Measurement

Our measure of ability to judge poetry is based on an instrument developed by Trabue and Abott in 1920[7] and a very fascinating one it is. What the authors did was to collect a large set of poems ranging from *Mother Goose* to Milton and to construct "bad" versions of brief selections from each. In a systematic fashion they created for each poem: a) a version sentimentalized in wording, b) a version which was systematically flattened to make it "matter-of-fact," and c) a metrically damaged version. These were then submitted to a panel of "experts" who, as one might expect, often preferred the damaged version to the original, but those poems on which there was consensus were preserved. The final instrument consisted of a test set of poems which was administered to samples of respondents of different educational levels (the authors were interested in elementary education, so a large part of their sample was from grade and high schools) who were asked to pick the version which they preferred.

We were unable to locate, even with the kind assistance of Dr. Trabue and the long distance telephone, a complete set of the poems, so we used in our study the four which appeared in the original publication. For each we gave the original, the sentimental, and the matter-of-fact version. Unfortunately, since the publication of the original study, Sandburg's "Fog" has been embalmed in so many high school textbooks that it is not a fair test, since many people know the correct version by rote. However, 23 per cent of our sample managed to get it wrong, so we kept it in the analysis. The poems used and the instructions in the schedule are reproduced on pp. 81-84.

In subjecting the test results to more intensive examination, we first looked at the intercorrelations among respondents' choices for the four poems. Although, given our large sample, some of the relationships are "statistically significant," they are all so low as to suggest either that the poems measure four different dimensions of poetic sophistication, or else an awful lot of people are guessing. Since data like these will not make

---

[7] M. R. Trabue and Allen Abott, "A Measure of Ability to Judge Poetry." *Teacher's College Record*, Vol. XXII, March, 1921.

satisfactory scales, we merely dichotomized the respondents into a high and low group — those who got three or four correct versus, those who got zero, one, or two correct. This dichotomization was used in much of the analysis which follows.

By way of further exploration of the test results we shall consider four separate questions: 1) How do Great Books participants compare with the original authors' norms? 2) How do scores on poetry, musical sophistication, and knowledge relate to each other? 3) What sorts of people in the program are better and poorer judges of poetry?, and 4) Does continued exposure to the program increase poetic discrimination?

Great Books Participants vs. Original Test Subjects

Trabue and Abott report norms for each specific poem for fairly large numbers of students ranging from grade school to graduate study in English. Although the data were not obtained from a probability sample and are almost 40 years old, they are, nevertheless, probably the only good data existing on poetic sensitivity in the United States. In any case, a comparison of the scores of our respondents with the responses of these original subjects may be somewhat illuminating. To make the two sets of responses comparable, however, it was necessary for us to apply a corrective factor to the scores of the Great Books participants. The original study presented four versions of each poem to each respondent, whereas we used only three versions. In the original research, therefore, respondents on the average could be expected to get 25 per cent of the poems right by sheer guesswork, while in our study, guess work could get 33 per cent right. Comparability of the two sets of data was achieved by dividing the proportion who picked the correct version for each poem by the chance expectation. For the original materials the chance expectation was .250; for Great Books, .333. Thus if .420 Great Books participants got a certain poem right they would get an index value of 1.26, which means that 1.26 times as many got it right as would have from sheer guessing. Any value greater than 1.00 then indicates the superiority of the respondents over a pair of dice. The resulting comparative scores are given by educational level in the table on the following page.

Great Books participants were consistently more likely to get "Fog" right, but for poems which are not widely known, there was little difference between the scores of the two groups. If anything, within a roughly comparable educational level, the Great Books participant was a little less likely to pick the correct version. Excluding "Fog," there were 15 comparisons, 12 of which favored the original sample, three of which favored the Great Books participants. At least three of the 12 are unfair, for in the "graduate" group the comparison is between graduate students in English in the original sample, and graduate students in a number of fields in Great Books. We should note, however, that Great Books graduate students generally did less well than Trabue's undergraduates so the difference is not merely one of graduate training in the field of English.

TABLE 43

Index of Correct Poetry Choices by Education and Specific Poem,
Great Books and Original Study Sample

Poem	Sample	Education*					
		High School	Post High School Non-College		College		Graduate
		III	IV	I	II	III-IV	
Milton	Trabue	0.50	0.80	0.77	0.86	1.17	1.79
	Great Books	0.73	0.82	0.76	0.74	0.95	0.96
House Fear	Trabue	0.71	1.31	1.53	1.89	1.94	2.67
	Great Books	0.97	1.05	0.64	1.09	1.26	1.16
Sea Shell	Trabue	1.60	2.00	2.37	2.04	2.22	2.54
	Great Books	1.00	1.44	1.52	1.70	1.60	1.52
Fog	Trabue	0.53	0.65	1.38	1.46	1.54	1.93
	Great Books	1.71	1.87	2.24	2.22	2.49	2.43

* We worked out the following rough equivalents to Trabue's years of school: For Great Books, 11th grade or less (N=37) was set equivalent to third year high; high school graduate (N=146) was set equivalent to fourth year high; post high, non-college (N=104) was inserted between high school and college and has no direct comparison; part college (N=423) was set equivalent to college II; college graduate (N=411) was set equivalent to III-IV; and graduate work (N=672) was compared with graduate work. The numbers of cases in Trabue's samples, reading from left to right along the top of the table are: 288, 284, 228, 178, 202, and 261.

On the whole, though, the Great Books participants were neither clearly superior nor inferior to the original study group (which was probably, of course, quite select itself, in that the respondents came from schools well above the national average).

Comparison of Poetry Test Results with Other Test Results

Before directing our attention to internal differences in poetic acuity, we should consider the interrelationships of our set of cultural "tests."

The three basic measures of high cultural aptitude in our study are: 1) the picture test of knowledge of the liberal arts and humanities, 2) the musical sophistication scale, and 3) the poetry test. We can begin by asking about their statistical relationships with each other. There are two good reasons for this. First, if they are highly related, we will have to use the other two as "controls" before we can really understand whether the third has a genuine or spurious relationship with such variables as sex, education, religion, and so on. A somewhat more interesting reason, though, is this: throughout our study we have had a continuing interest in describing the intellectual and cultural orientations of the people in Great Books. We are interested in what they know, what they read, and what they are interested in. Each of these questions is treated in separate places in our study. There is, however, a more general question of how these cultural interests and abilities hang together. Do people who do well on one test also tend to do well on another, or are there "specialists" who focus on one area and not on another? The problem is a genuine one for those interested in liberal adult education, for the implicit assumption of such people is that it is possible to develop a "well-rounded" person who is interested in a wide variety of aspects of high culture. We don't propose to decide here and now whether it is possible to develop a well-rounded person, but we do hope to examine the pattern of relationships for our three tests.

To begin with, we could advance a number of hypotheses. Perhaps music and poetry correlate strongly because they are both "esthetic," contrasted with the cartoon test. Perhaps, however, poetry and cartoons are closely associated because both are verbal, while music is an auditory phenomenon. Or perhaps cartoon scores and music will be highly congruent because, with the growth of education and the rise of the record player, both are more widely "propagated" than poetry.

Let us look at the correlations. In Table 44 we see the "Q" coefficients of music, poetry, and cartoon scores. Both poetry and music have positive relationships with the knowledge measure, but they are independent of each other. In other words, people who are musically sophisticated or good judges of poetry will tend to have pretty high knowledge scores, but there is no way of predicting from music to poetry or from poetry to music.

TABLE 44

Associations Among Poetry, Music, and. Picture Scores

Correlates	Music	Pictures	Poetry
Music		.492	.033
Cartoons	.492		.215
Poetry	.033	.215	

The implication of these findings is that there is no "esthetic type" to be found here; rather, within a given level of knowledge of the whole range of culture, some people cultivate musical sensitivity, some cultivate poetry, some neither — but there is no relationship between excellence in the two areas of esthetics.

These ruminations, in turn, suggest that the most fruitful approach to the problem of locating the poetically sensitive is to consider a typology of high cultural emphasis rather than just looking for good and bad judges of the poems. Table 45 distributes the cases in our basic framework.

TABLE 45

Distribution of Cases in Typology of Cultural Abilities

Knowledge	Musical Sophistication	Poetry Skill	
		High	Low
High	High	153	302
	Low	135	263
Low	High	48	146
	Low	150	425

Now, when we look at the relationship between a given background variable and the typology we can ask a number of questions:

1) Is the variable related to knowledge, regardless of type of esthetic interest?

2) Is the variable related to music as an area of esthetic specialization, independent of its relationship to general cultural knowledge?

3) Is the variable related to poetry as an area of esthetic specialization, independent of its relationship to general cultural knowledge?

4) Is the variable related to both types of esthetic specialization, independent of its relationship to general cultural knowledge?

We examined correlations between abilities and a number of variables, with results which are summarized in the following table.

TABLE 46

Summary of Correlates of Cultural Typology

Characteristic	Consistent Relationship with		
	Knowledge	Music	Poetry
1. Education	Yes	Yes	—
2. Self-Conception	Yes	Yes	—
3. Sex	Yes	—	Yes
4. Party Preference	Yes	Yes	—
5. Church Attendance	Yes	Yes	Yes
6. Generation	—	Yes	Yes
7. Status of Household Head	Yes	—	—
8. Age	—	—	?
9. "Housewives"	—	—	—
10. Community	—	Yes	—
11. Catholics	—	Yes	?
12. Jews	Yes	Yes	?

As we suspected, the pattern is different for the three types of cultural emphasis. In only one case, church attendance, does a given variable relate to all three tests, and in that one the correlations are in *opposite* directions for different cultural measures.

Since we have considered the correlates of knowledge scores previously, we shall not repeat them here, but concentrate on music and poetry.

Regardless of their level of general cultural knowledge and their ability to judge poetry, people high on musical sophistication tend disproportionately to be: 1) Highly educated, 2) Self-defined intellectuals, 3) Democrats, 4) *Infrequent* church attenders, 5) Foreign born or the children of foreign born, 6) Residents of very large cities, 7) Non-Catholic, and 8) Jewish. Now, our number of cases is becoming too small to disentangle the relative contributions of these eight separate characteristics to musical sophistication, but it is clear that they make a lot of sociological sense. What these eight variables describe is the highly urban "intellectual," or to put it another way, what we have here is the 1956 Adlai Stevenson vote.

When we turn to the poetically sophisticated, we find that regardless of their level of knowledge and their musical sophistication, they tend disproportionately to be: 1) Women, 2) *Frequent* church attenders, and 3) Native born and children of native born parents. Somewhat less consistently, they tend to be: 4) Younger, 5) Roman Catholics, and 6) Non-Jewish. The complex which these variables describe is much less clear-cut than that suggested by the correlates of musical sophistication. With the exception of age, these characteristics suggest not a cultural type, but rather a temperament, which is difficult to put into words but might be suggested by phrases like "culturally conservative," this time using the sociological rather than popular sense of the word "cultural."

Regardless of the names we choose to give these packages of characteristics, it is clear that we will be unable to order our respondents in a simple ranking in terms of their mastery of the elements of liberal arts and knowledge. Neither will we be able to think of a simple distinction between the "bookish" and the "arty," for within the esthetic area, it appears that the type of specialization is both statistically independent and related to very different sets of social characteristics.

Exposure to Great Books and Poetry Scores

We began with the question of whether continued exposure to verse in the readings and to the esthetic discussions of the group result in increased poetic sensitivity. Having set the poetry test in the context of the original sample group and differences among the participants, we are ready to attack the problem directly. In Table 47 we see the proportion scoring high on the test, by exposure group, controlling for drop-out.

Table 47 provides no evidence that poetic sensitivity flowers with increased years in Great Books, the trends being inconsistent and statistically unreliable.

We have only two comments to make on this negative finding. First, from our previous analysis, it would appear that the sort of characteristics which are associated with high poetry scores are not the salient characteristics of Great Books participants. We remember from our earlier analysis that motivation appears to be a crucial determinant of "effect" and the motivation to "improve my taste in fiction and poetry" is mentioned by only 24 per cent of the respondents, not all of whom would necessarily give equal weights to fiction and to poetry.

TABLE 47

Exposure and Poetry Scores, Controlling for Drop-Out
Per cent high on poetry test

1957 Exposure (years)	1958 Status		
	Dropped	Continued	Total
3+	35 (94)	25 (330)	27 (424)
1 and 2	29 (135)	31 (406)	30 (541)
0	25 (298)	26 (348)	25 (646)
	(Base N in parentheses)		

Second, other studies indicate that all programs have great difficulty in teaching poetic sensitivity. We remember that Trabue's graduate students in English didn't do quite *twice* as well as guessing on the Milton selection, which is probably the most distinguished piece of verse in the lot.

We would probably consider Cambridge University as a fairly effective educational institution. In 1929 I. A. Richards, the literary critic, published the results of an informal experiment, analogous in form to our study.[8] He gave untitled poems to advanced undergraduates for their comments, and from their protocols evaluated the students' poetic sensitivity. His own comments are judicial and calm, but the results have been more mordantly summarized by Stanley Edgar Hyman:

"What the protocols reveal, by and large, is probably the most shocking picture, exhaustively documented, of the general reading of poetry ever presented. Perhaps the most frightening single thing Richards got was evidence that his students (and, presumably, all but a few particularly qualified readers and poets) lean absolutely on the authority of the writer's name, and their sense of its rank in the pantheon, as a crutch." [9]

Richards' own conclusions may serve well for us.[10]

"It is *not* inevitable, or in the nature of things, that poetry should seem such a remote, mysterious, unmanageable thing to so large a majority of readers. The deficiencies so noticeable in the protocol writers (and, if we could be franker with ourselves, in our reading) are not native, inalterable defects in the average human mind. They are due in a large degree to mistakes that can be avoided, and to bad training. In fact, does anyone ever receive any useful training in this matter?"

[8] I. A. Richards, *Practical Criticism: A Study of Literary Judgment*, London: Routledge & Kegan Paul, Ltd., 1929.
[9] Stanley Edgar Hyman, *The Armed Vision: A Study in the Methods of Modern Literary Criticism*, revised and abridged by the author. New York: Vintage Books, 1955, p. 291.
[10] Richards, *op. cit.*, p. 309.

POEMS USED IN THE SCHEDULE

POETRY

Listed below and on the following pages are four poems. For each, three versions are given. Please check the version which you prefer as poetry.

Poem 1

A.
Tender, tender Sea Shell,
Wilt thou sing me, please,
Of thy happy, happy home
'Neath the tropic trees?
Ah, the coral islands!
Ah, the wondrous fish!
For such a song I'd give thee, dear,
Whate'er a Shell could wish.

B.
Sea Shell, please sing me a song
Of ships and sailor-men;
Of strange kinds of birds and trees
On the Spanish Main:
Of fish and seaweed in the sea,
And whatever creature there may be, —
Sea Shell, please sing me a song!

C.
(Original)
Sea Shell, Sea Shell,
Sing me a song, Oh please!
A song of ships and sailor men,
Of parrots and tropical trees.
Of islands lost in the Spanish Main
Which no man ever may find again,
Of fishes and coral under the waves,
And sea-horses stabled in great green caves —
Sea Shell, Sea Shell
Sing me a song, Oh please!

Poem 2

A.   Let there be Light, said God, and lo! the Light
Sprung from Tithonus' bed in darksome gloom,
Deck'd her fair form in garments rich and rare
And scattered smiles along the mournful sky.
Her chariot of the Sun not yet created,
Upon a cloud the nymph ethereal rode,
And when the cloud wept raindrops down, she flung
Comforting rainbows from her shining tent.

B.   Let there be light, said God, and forthwith Light
(Original) Ethereal, first of things, quintessence pure,
Sprung from the Deep, and from her native east
To journey through the airy gloom began,
Spher'd in a radiant cloud, for yet the Sun
Was not; she in a cloudy tabernacle
Sojourn'd the while. God saw the Light was good.

C.   And God said, "Let Light be," and there was Light
The first ethereal created thing
To being sprang, and daily from the east
Began to travel through the darksome air;
Until the golden sun should be created
She sojourn'd in a radiant, shining cloud.
God look'd upon the Light and it was good.

Poem 3

A.   This was the routine they learned
        Always at night when they returned
        To lamps unlighted and fires gone gray
        When they had been away all day.
        They learned to build the fire up quick
        With half a split-up kindling stick —
        And knowing how the cat delights
        To sleep indoors by the fire of nights,
        They learned to leave the house door wide
        For fear they might leave her shut outside.

B.   Always — I tell you this they learned —
(Original) Always at night when they returned
        To the lonely house from far away
        To lamps unlighted and fire gone gray,
        They learned to rattle the lock and key
        To give whatever might chance to be
        Warning and time to be off in flight:
        And preferring the out- to the in-door night,
        They learned to leave the house-door wide,
        Until they had lit the lamp inside.

C.   Always their hearts would thrill with fear
        When at dead of night they again drew near
        To the dismal, lonely, dark abode
        Where not a glimmer of lamp-light showed.
        Trembling, they turned the lock and key
        With pallid face and shaking knee.
        There was nothing to cause their fright,
        But they felt more safe in the out-door night!
        So they left the house-door open wide,
        And fell in a faint on the floor inside.

Poem 4

A.

Who sends the fog
so still and gray?
I fondly ask.
And Echo answers,
"E'en the same all-seeing Eye
that sends the still, gray cat."

B.

The Fog is like a maltese cat,
it is so gray and still,
and like a cat it creeps
about the city streets.
How gray it is! How cat-like!
Especially when it steals away,
Just like a cat.

C.
(Original)

The fog comes
on little cat feet.
It sits looking
over harbor and city
on silent haunches
and then moves on.

Reading

Compared to the American public in general, or to the public of their own educational level as studied in national surveys, Great Books participants are outstanding as readers.

In 1945 NORC, on behalf of the American Library Association, surveyed the reading habits of a sample of adults in 17 cities.[11] Of the people in this sample who had attended college, 41 per cent reported that they spent seven or more hours a week in reading books. Because we separated reading into "light" and "serious" rather than into the format of the material read, we do not have an exactly comparable question; however, 80 per cent of the Great Books respondents spend at least 7 hours a week on their total reading, and 50 per cent spend 11 or more hours a week in reading. Even if one assumes that almost a third of their total reading time is spent on newspapers and periodicals, the Great Books participants have a higher percentage who spend at least an hour a day reading books than does the college segment of the urban public surveyed by NORC.

Going from numbers to level of taste and difficulty, one immediately loses any easily-agreed-upon basis of judgment. We can, however, report the general impression gained from reading the lists of books which the participants reported as among the "particularly worthwhile" ones which they had read in the past year (aside from the Great Books readings). None, or almost none, of the books were of a "lowbrow" sort, and only a few were highly popular historical novels. Among the less difficult books listed, Kennedy's *Profiles in Courage,* several books by Erich Fromm, *By Love Possessed,* widely read popular religious books, and *The Diary of Anne Frank* are fairly typical.

Very seriously intellectual books are almost as completely missing as wholly superficial ones, however. Serious philosophy and criticism were extreme rarities, and literary works of the first rank were not very common. It is, of course, possible that the time and attention devoted to the Great Books reading turned the participants' attention away from the more difficult books which they might otherwise have read, but one does not come away from the questionnaires with the impression that such is the case.

When one turns to magazine-reading, other studies which are comparable in their samples have asked questions which are too different to provide material for useful comparisons. When one compares the per cent of Great Books entrants who reported themselves as regular or occasional [12] readers of certain magazines with general knowledge of the circulation of

---

[11] National Opinion Research Center, *What . . . Where . . . Why . . . Do People Read?,* Report No. 28 (1945), p. 6.

[12] Given the way that the magazine question was set up, the answer "Occasionally" implies more frequent reading than does "Seldom" and approaches "fairly regularly" in meaning.

the magazines, however, he gets at least a rough picture of the relative magazine-reading habits of Great Books members.

Table 48 gives the percentages of Great Books entrants who classed themselves as regular or occasional readers of a selected list of magazines, here presented in order of their popularity rank among the participants.

TABLE 48

Magazine-Reading Habits of Great Books Entrants
Selected magazines

Magazine	Per cent of respondents who read regularly or occasionally
Time	87
The Reader's Digest	69
The New Yorker	69
The Saturday Evening Post	59
Saturday Review	49
Harper's	45
Scientific American	22
The New Republic	18
Art News	8
High Fidelity	7
The Partisan Review	4
	(N = 1,759)

When one considers the relative circulation of *The Saturday Evening Post* and the *Saturday Review,* or that of *The New Yorker* and *The Reader's Digest,* or even that of *Time* and *The New Republic* or *Scientific American,* it appears safe to say that Great Books entrants read a disproportionate number of serious or sophisticated magazines. Quite obviously, however, most of them do not exclude such highly popular magazines as *The Reader's Digest* and *The Saturday Evening Post* from their reading.

The amount of one's reading and its level of difficulty may be two very different matters. We have two indications of the reading level of Great Books participants: their own list of worthwhile books read in the past year, and their pattern of magazine-reading from a list presented in the questionnaire.

Books

The relevant question on book-reading asked: "What book or books — outside of the Great Books readings — which you read in the last year impressed you as particularly worthwhile?" Six hundred and nine failed to list any books, and an additional 142 listed books which were impossible to classify, 17 including only the Bible and the rest listing books dealing with hobbies, religious devotions, or special technical interests. Eleven hundred and fifty-eight people, however, did list books which could be classified as fiction or non-fiction and roughly rated as to level of difficulty or taste. We cannot make serious claims of scientific objectivity in the rating of the books as more and less difficult, but can say that the division was made thoughtfully by the study director and spot-checked for agreement by another staff member. People were classified on the basis of whether their list of "worthwhile books" included only the more difficult ones, only less difficult ones, or a mixture. To give the reader an idea of the standards used, the lists below give some of the "particularly worthwhile" reading the participants listed and our classification of it.

More Difficult

> Barnett, *The Universe and Dr. Einstein*
> Camus, *The Fall*
> Ortega y Gasset, *Revolt of the Masses*
> Proust, *Remembrance of Things Past*
> Spinoza, *Ethics*
> Strindberg, *Dance of Death*

Less Difficult

> Cozzens, *By Love Possessed*
> Ferber, *Giant*
> Fromm, *The Art of Loving*
> Hulme, *The Nun's Story*
> Lindbergh, *Gift from the Sea*
> Marshall, *Mr. Jones, Meet the Master*

As the introductory summary has already noted, there were no listings of books of a really "lowbrow" sort. Romantic novels from the best-seller lists are about the bottom of the reading mentioned. The following table gives the distribution of respondents on the level of books listed.

TABLE 49

Percent of Participants Reading

Difficult Only	Mixture	Less Difficult Only	N
23	35	42	(1158)

As a look at the table shows, 58 per cent of the respondents who listed classifiable books included one or more which fell into the "difficult" category. Given the fact that the participants were asked to list books which they had found particularly worthwhile, this distribution does not suggest that their serious reading is on an extremely high level of difficulty.

Whether this level relates to total hours of reading is another question. Table 50 shows the distribution of each total reading group on the level of the worthwhile books reported.

TABLE 50

Level of Difficulty of "Worthwhile" Books Listed by Respondents, by Respondents' Total Weekly Hours of Reading

Per cent in each total reading group reporting books of each level

Level of Books	Total Hours Reading		
	1-7	8-14	15 or more
Some or all "difficult"	56	54	63
None "difficult"	44	46	37
	100 (218)	100 (475)	100 (271)

The proportion of people who include some "difficult" works in their lists of worthwhile books is somewhat higher among the people who do the most reading.

Magazines

A second and different measure of level of reading is a scale constructed from the answers to the question on magazines read. The respondents were presented with the list of magazines shown in Table 48 and asked to check whether they read them regularly, occasionally, or seldom, had heard of them but never read them, or had never heard of them. Within this pattern of choice, occasional reading was combined with regular reading in the construction of the scale described below.

The association between reading each magazine and each of the other magazines, regularly or occasionally, was measured by calculating the Q values. Table 51 gives the matrix of intercorrelations. The general point of the table is that the association declines as the magazines are farther apart from each other in the listing. There is no statistical magic in this; the magazines have been listed in the order which gives the effect. Such listing is possible, however, only if the magazines have in fact the underlying pattern of relationship. Four periodicals, *Gadfly* (the "house organ" of the Great Books program) and three appealing to more or less special interests, did not fit into the scale, although the pattern suggests that *Art News, Scientific American,* and *High Fidelity* do belong toward the more "difficult" end of the scale. The others showed a pattern of relationship which strongly suggests that the pattern classifies readers on the basis of the level of seriousness of their typical magazine-reading. Reading across the top line as an example, one sees that people who read *The Reader's Digest* are quite likely to read

The Saturday Evening Post and moderately likely to read *Time.* It is somewhat unlikely that they read *The New Yorker, Harper's, Saturday Review,* or *The New Republic,* and more unlikely that they read *The Partisan Review.*

TABLE 51

Magazine-Reading Intercorrelations

(Based on "read regularly" and "read occasionally")

	Reader's Digest	Sat. Eve. Post	Time	New Yorker	Harper's	Sat. Review	New Republic	Partisan Review
Reader's Digest ..	—	.768	.463	−.247	−.262	−.322	−.271	−.480
Sat. Eve. Post....	.768	—	.491	.050	−.053	−.033	−.198	−.334
Time	.463	.491	—	.307	−.068	.075	−.032	−.126
New Yorker	−.247	.050	.307	—	.572	.507	.426	.370
Harper's	−.262	−.053	−.068	.572	—	.621	.630	.558
Sat. Review	−.322	−.033	.075	.507	.621	—	.597	.704
New Republic ...	−.271	−.198	−.032	.426	.630	.597	—	.763
Partisan Review .	−.480	−.334	−.126	.370	.558	.704	.763	—

On the basis of the associations which the magazines showed, five were selected arbitrarily for use in a scale of the level of magazine reading: *The Reader's Digest, The New Yorker* OR *Harper's,* and *The New Republic* OR *The Partisan Review.* The fact that this selection of magazines represents the range of the respondents' magazine-reading is indicated by the fact that only 130 of the 1900 people who answered the questions on magazines cannot be included in the scale. The distribution of the respondents whose magazine-reading could be scaled is indicated in Table 52. A plus-sign indicates regular or occasional reading, and a minus-sign anything less than that.

TABLE 52

Distribution of Respondents on Scale of Magazine-Reading

Reader's Digest	New Yorker OR Harper's	New Republic OR Partisan Review	Per Cent of Respondents	Scale Score
+	−	−	21	I
+	+	−	38	II
−	+	−	22	III
−	+	+	9	IV
−	−	+	1	V
+	+	+	8	Ambiguous
+	−	+	1	Ambiguous
			(N=1770)	

+ indicates regular or occasional reading
− indicates less frequent reading, including not reading

While only about one-fifth of the respondents show magazine-reading only at *The Reader's Digest* level of difficulty, only one per cent include only *The New Republic* or *The Partisan Review* in their reading. Like the finding on the level of books reported as particularly worthwhile, the pattern of magazine-reading suggests that Great Books participants tend to read magazines of a middle level of difficulty, with few limiting themselves to the completely popular magazines on the list and few including those of more than middling seriousness.

When one looks at the relationship between total time spent on reading and level of magazine-reading, he sees the picture presented below.

TABLE 53

Total Weekly Hours of Reading and Level of Magazine-Reading

Per cent of respondents in each total weekly reading hours group who report each level of magazine-reading

Magazine Scale Scores	Total Hours Reading		
	1-7 hours	8-14 hours	15 or more hours
IV & V	15	18	26
III	23	24	21
II	38	40	38
I	24	18	15
N	(340)	(677)	(364)

In general, the same finding applies to magazine-reading as applied to worthwhile books reported: there is a very slight tendency for more extensive readers to have a higher proportion of people who include difficult material in their reading.

The differences in the percentages of people falling in the top category on book- as compared with magazine-reading tempt one to make comparisons, but the data should not be used in this way. The books include only those which the respondents listed as the particularly worthwhile ones read in the preceding year, while the magazines represent unevaluated reading. It is not surprising that the report on books includes a much higher proportion of people falling in the top category than does the report on magazines.

Combined Level of Reading

Although the choices do, thus, reflect different things — on books, those considered particularly worthwhile, and on magazines, habitual reading — some comparison (and later combination) seems possible. Table 54 divides the respondents who listed codable books on the basis of including or not including some "difficult" books in their lists, and presents the distribution of each group on level of magazine-reading.

TABLE 54

Level of "Worthwhile" Books Reported by Respondents,
by Respondents' Level of Magazine-Reading

Magazine-Reading Scale-Score	Respondents Who Included "Difficult" Books in Their List of Worthwhile Books	Respondents Who Did Not Include Any "Difficult" Books
IV & V	24 ⎫	18 ⎫
III	31 ⎭ 55%	18 ⎭ 36%
II	31 ⎫	43 ⎫
I	14 ⎭ 45%	21 ⎭ 64%
	100%	100%
N	(619)	(463)

There is evidently a tendency for the listers of difficult books to read more difficult magazines, but the categories are far from cleanly divided.

Although the book and magazine levels show only a slight relationship — in fact, because they do — there seems to be some use in combining them. Neither alone is a representative measure of reading level, and yet, people who read more difficult material in books but not in magazines, or vice versa, may have different characteristics from people who do not read more difficult material in either books or magazines. On this line of reasoning, the participants were classified according to the general reading-level scale shown in Table 55.

TABLE 55

Distribution of Participants on General Reading-Level Scale

Category	Per cent
Include both "difficult" books and "difficult" magazines	9
Include "difficult" books only	29
Include "difficult" magazines only	10
Include no "difficult" material but some middle-level magazines	23
Include no "difficult" material and only the least difficult magazines	29
	(N=1,639)

(Respondents who reported no books were classified by their level of magazine reading.)

Having looked at patterns of reading in general, we are now ready to ask whether continued exposure to Great Books is associated with differences in reading, outside of the reading required for the discussions. Our report has already shown some of the effects associated with continued exposure to the Great Books themselves. Now, however, let us consider whether there is a transfer effect on other reading patterns.

We can begin by looking at "quantity," the total hours of reading reported.

The reader will remember that we asked for quantity estimates for three types of reading, outside of professional or job reading — reading for relaxation, preparation for Great Books, and serious reading. Total number of hours spent for reading does increase both in our cross-sectional comparisons and also in our drop-out control tables; however, the change is selective, relaxation reading remaining constant. Here are the tables for the other two types:

TABLE 56

Exposure and Serious Reading, Controlling for Drop-Outs
Per cent spending three or more hours per week on serious reading

1957 Exposure (years)	1958 Status		
	Dropped	Continued	Total
3+	71 (76)	67 (296)	68 (372)
1 and 2	55 (120)	58 (360)	57 (480)
0	57 (258)	59 (307)	58 (565)
	(Base N in parentheses)		

TABLE 57

Exposure and Great Books Reading, Controlling for Drop-Outs
Per cent spending three or more hours per week on Great Books preparation

1957 Exposure (years)	1958 Status		
	Dropped	Continued	Total
3+	73 (88)	74 (317)	73 (405)
1 and 2	60 (129)	65 (387)	63 (516)
0	51 (279)	57 (334)	54 (613)
	(Base N in parentheses)		

The key comparisons in Table 56, the ones which give us an estimate of changes uncontaminated by drop-outs, indicate an increase in serious reading in the advanced group as compared with the middle exposure group ($p < .01$), but no difference between the beginning and middle exposure participants. Therefore, we may infer that *after some time in the program* there is a spreading seriousness of reading. Table 57 corroborates our impression that this is not at the expense of reading for the program, for while the increase between 0 and 1-2 is not statistically reliable, the increase between the middle- and advanced-exposure groups is statistically reliable ($p < .01$). Thus, the most advanced participants tend to report significantly more hours per week spent on Great Books and also on serious reading outside the program. To put it another way, it appears that continued participation in Great Books expands the total quantity of reading by increasing the serious reading time, without leading to a contraction in reading for relaxation.

When we say that Great Books participation leads to *more* serious reading, we have not demonstrated that it also produces more *serious* reading. In fact, our crude indices of quality fail to show any consistent difference (using our combined book-and-magazine index as well as its separate components) in the seriousness of the reading materials reported in different exposure groups. It may be that our index is poor, or it may be that the effect of the program is to increase the quantity of serious reading for the advanced-year member without affecting his (or, rather, it should probably be "her") qualitative degree of level of difficulty.

Summary

In this chapter we have examined our survey's data on the relationship between exposure to the program and selected aspects of the members' intellectual lives. The clearest and strongest effect was a definite increase in knowledge of the liberal arts, as measured by a quiz taken by the members. In the area of reading, we found the respondents to be characterized by a consistent pattern of "middlebrow" reading tastes. Our evidence suggests that, in the advanced years, the program does lead to a quantitative increase in hours per week spent on serious reading, both of Great Books assignments and of self-chosen materials, but that the level of difficulty of the respondents' readings is not related to exposure. Neither of our measures of esthetic taste — musical sophistication and ability to judge poetry — showed any relationship to exposure.

Thus, in the area which is an overt program goal — exposure to Great Books themselves — rather strong increases have been demonstrated. As, however, we move to consider possible intellectual side effects, we find less evidence of change.

CHAPTER TWO

VALUES, IDEOLOGIES, AND COMMUNITY INVOLVEMENT

Although we have used our statistical scalpel at great length on the armchair aspects of Great Books effects, it is now time to consider the fact that the participants not only read books but also read ideas. In fact, our previous analysis suggests that it is not from the esthetic, but from the intellectual content of the readings that the major effects of the program stem. Therefore, in this chapter we shall look for possible effects in the areas of basic values, of ideological positions regarding religion and politics, and of involvement in local community affairs.

Values and Ideologies

With the exception of the verse discussed in Chapter I of Part C and some highly abstract works, such as Euclid, a large proportion of the Great Books readings can be thought of as discourses in social and political values

— that is, statements on what is preferable and desirable in the areas of political organization, religion, and social relationships. We need only think of Marx, St. Thomas, Thoreau, Mill, Adam Smith, Plato, and Aristotle to document this point.

Our impression is that the readings themselves betray no "party line," except that, as implied in the definition of the program, twentieth-century thought receives less stress. The participants read a range of political thought from Marx to Mill, and the Christian theologians (St. Thomas and St. Augustine) are counter-balanced by Freud, Darwin, Nietzsche, and a large number of classical "pagans."

Out of this welter of value positions, one wonders whether certain ones "take" better than others, and whether continued participation in the program is associated with any specific leanings on the social and political questions which loom so large in the readings.

Subjective Reports

We can begin by asking the respondents whether they *think* they have changed in their basic positions. A pretty good index can be derived from the following two questions:

"Since you began Great Books have there been any particular authors or schools of thought which you once disliked, but now find more aceptable? If 'yes,' which ones?"

"Since you began Great Books are there any particular authors or schools of thought which you once accepted, but now find less aceptable? If 'yes,' which ones?"

When we cross-tabulate these two questions for the entire sample, we get the following:

TABLE 58

Reported Changes in Acceptance of Particular Schools of Thought

More Acceptable	Less Acceptable		Total
	Yes	No	
Yes	6%	21%	27%
No	6	66	72
	12%	87%	99%
	(N=1,507)		

Over-all, we find 27 per cent reporting one or more authors or schools of thought found to be more acceptable; 12 per cent reporting some area as less acceptable; and when the two are considered together, we find 33 per cent reporting some form of change and 66 per cent reporting no change. The major pattern of change appears to be that of increasing one's likes without abandoning any previously admired position, this pattern being almost twice as common as the other two types of change combined. Thus, about one-third of the respondents do report some type of change of the sort we are exploring in this chapter.

As one would expect, the longer one has been in the program, the more likely he is to report such a change, 79 per cent reporting no change in the first year, 67 per cent in the middle group, and 44 per cent in the advanced years.

Table 59 shows the proportion reporting "no change" for various sub-groups, controlling for exposure.

TABLE 59

Sub-Group Differences in Acceptance Pattern
Per cent reporting no change

	Years of Exposure		
	0	1 and 2	3 or more
Education:			
No college	87 (93)	64 (67)	40 (57)
Part college and A.B.	78 (281)	65 (243)	43 (155)
Graduate study	77 (236)	70 (191)	44 (148)
Sex:			
Male	78 (232)	72 (198)	46 (166)
Female	79 (400)	64 (308)	42 (203)
Age:			
Under 35	79 (299)	64 (212)	46 (65)
35-44	81 (178)	66 (154)	37 (130)
45 or more	74 (149)	71 (135)	48 (175)
Impact:			
High	73 (173)	58 (209)	39 (222)
Low	81 (435)	74 (285)	51 (141)
Religion:			
Protestant	79 (385)	68 (277)	41 (207)
Catholic	82 (68)	80 (50)	47 (19)
Jewish	76 (84)	65 (72)	52 (58)
None	74 (57)	55 (67)	39 (59)
	(Base N in parentheses)		

None of the sub-group differences is terribly strong, but several deserve a few words of comment. Educational trends are slight, but they show an increasing reversal. In the first year, those with lower education are more likely to report a change, but in the advanced years, more changers (i.e., in terms of Table 59, non-non-changers) are found in the higher educational levels. It may be that the person with lower education experiences a quicker immediate impact but that over the long haul more changers are found among those of higher education. There is a slight but consistent sex difference in favor of the women, which is probably not an artifact of the educational difference in the sexes, since it appears in all three exposure groups, while the educational difference reverses after the first year. There is no consistent age difference. With the exception of the Jews in the advanced years, there does appear to be a slight but consistent religious difference. On the whole, Catholics are least likely to report a change, Protestants next least likely, Jews somewhat more likely to report a change, and "Nones" the most likely to report some change.

With these findings in mind, let us now turn to the question of the *content* of these changes.

Specific Values and Ideologies

The changes in values and ideologies suggested by the above analysis could be of two different types. One type could be that of a high "turn-over" in individuals, but little net effect. The other could be that of high turnover in individuals, with an over-all direction. Table 60 gives a hypothetical example of these two types of change.

TABLE 60

Hypothetical Types of Change

		A. Time 2					B. Time 2		
		X	Y				X	Y	
	X	25	25	50		X	0	50	50
Time 1					Time 1				
	Y	25	25	50		Y	0	50	50
		50	50	100			0	100	100

Let us think of two value positions, X and Y, and the same population measured at two times (Time 1 and Time 2). In both situations, A and B, 50 people, or half of the population, have changed their position on the values. In Situation A, however, the changes cancel each other out, 25 people moving from X to Y, and 25 from Y to X, leaving the proportions of adherents of X and Y the same. In Situation B, all 50 shifted from X to Y, but the *proportion* of Y's shifts from 50 per cent at Time 1 to 100 per cent at Time 2.

Now, we can conclude from the previous analysis that the turnover may be fairly high in Great Books, but since we do not have measures on the same person at two different times, we will be unable to detect any A-like situations. Therefore, when we turn to specific content, we compare beginning and advanced participants to look for "net effects" and can tell little from our data about "gross" rates of change, except for the subjective materials reported above.

We shall examine four types of values here. We shall begin with the value instrument developed by Morris, to which we have already referred in Part A. We shall then turn to some specific social and intellectual values. Next we shall examine religious orientations, and, finally, materials on political ideology.

Morris Values

The Morris value vignettes, as the reader of Part A will remember, consist of four brief statements of basic value positions which we described with the labels of "Groupyness," "Activity," "Hedonism," and "Contemplation." At that time we remarked that the participants seemed to be characterized by high adherence to what might be called modal middle-class values of groupyness and activity, and lesser adherence to the deviant values of hedonism or contemplation. Let us now see whether continued participation in Great Books is associated with any differences in these patterns.

TABLE 61

Morris Values

Per cent checking "Like very much" or
"Like quite a lot" by years of exposure

		Exposure	
Value	0	1 and 2	3 or more
Groupyness	46 (711)	43 (550)	51 (427)
Activity	38 (704)	32 (544)	36 (427)
Hedonism	23 (700)	28 (550)	25 (418)
Contemplation	18 (702)	19 (545)	22 (415)
	(Base N in parentheses)		

We see in Table 61 no differences either in the percentages or in the relative popularity of these values. This is not too surprising, as this measure was developed essentially for cross-cultural studies, and within a given culture, the range of variation is presumably quite small. Exposure to Great Books seems to show no "net" relationship with scores on these measures. Drop-out control tables show the same lack of trend.

Religious Systems

In an attempt to get at intellectual orientations toward religion, as well as denominational preference and attendance, we asked the following question:

"Below are twelve different systems of religious thought. In the column headed 'Most Congenial' please check the *three* systems which you find most congenial intellectually. In the column headed 'Least Congenial' please check the *three* systems which you find least congenial intellectually."

The following were then listed in alphabetical order:

Atheism
Agnosticism
Buddhism
Mysticism
Reform Judaism
Christian Science
"Fundamentalist" Protestantism
"Middle of the Road" Protestantism
Thomism
Orthodox Judaism
"Liberal" Protestantism
Mohammedanism.

We shall soon see that our drop-out control tables suggest a fairly consistent pattern of changes in intellectual orientations toward religion; however, we can interpret them more easily by noting some aspects of religious behavior which do *not* change. In the first place, the per cent checking "extremely important to me" in answer to the question, "Church-going aside, religious ideas and theological problems are . . . ," remains very close to 42 per cent in all exposure groups, among drop-outs and non-drop-outs. Likewise, the per cent attending church "regularly" or "fairly regularly" remains a constant slight majority across the board. The denominational picture, too, shows no simple trends. (There do appear to be some rather complex relationships between religious preference and adherence to the program, but since our groups tend to religious homogeneity, the failure of two or three individual discussion groups may explain them.)

We can summarize the findings on changes in intellectual orientations as follows:

I) Positions which become more congenial: (a) Mysticism, (b) Atheism, (c) Agnosticism, (d) "Liberal" Protestantism, and (e) Reform Judaism.

II) Positions which show no change: (a) Mohammedanism, and (b) Buddhism.

III) Positions which become less congenial: (a) Thomism, (b) "Middle of the Road" Protestantism, (c) Orthodox Judaism, (d) "Fundamentalist" Protestantism, and (e) Christian Science.

Now, not all of these differences are individually statistically reliable in each comparison, but each is either statistically significant for one comparison or for the total. Furthermore, the patterning of changes is quite clear.

We would suggest that the direction is as follows: There is a distinct tendency for exposure to Great Books to lead the participants toward a greater acceptance of more liberal, rational, and skeptical approaches toward religion. At the same time distinct limits on this process appear, since (a) there are no shifts toward religious viewpoints outside of the Judaeo-Christian tradition, (b) there is no decrease in religious concern *per se,* and (c) overt religious behavior does not appear to change. One way of viewing the matter would be that the religious changes are not those of abandoning or altering a fundamental religious stance, but rather they may be those of changing evaluations of *other* viewpoints. The general picture is not one of reversals or dramatic changes in religious ideas, but one of expansion of the breadth and scope of religious ideas which are considered within the pale, an expansion which is generally in the "liberal" rather than in the "orthodox" direction.

Political Ideologies

We didn't plan it that way, but, curiously, throughout our study political preferences have played an important part in the analyses. In independence of its relationships with such variables as education, age, and status, party preference has turned up as a correlate of motivations for joining the program, musical sophistication and poetic skill. Therefore, even aside from the fact that the readings in the program have a heavy political emphasis, we shall be interested in the question of whether political values, too, vary with exposure to Great Books.

The contemporary American political scene is a little too complicated to be covered by two questions in a survey, but in designing our study we felt that two important axes of political values today are the question of "civil liberties" and the question of "government control." Many political observers, of course, believe that in the late 1950's political ideologies have become considerably less important in a national scene dominated by questions of foreign policy and by technical economic and administrative issues which don't lend themselves to simple ideological polarities. Nevertheless, we felt that the questions of whether governmental activities have been extended too far or not far enough (the continuing question of where one stands *vis-à-vis* the New Deal), and whether a balance has been struck between the competing demands of civil liberties and national security (at one time the issue of "McCarthyism"), would still provide a basis of differentiation.

The specific items are:

GOVERNMENT

"In general, which of the following statements comes closest to expressing your basic position on government in the United States?"

There is too much government control today. Governmental activities should be cut back.

There is a lot of government control today, but, in general, it is called for by the needs of our society.

We need to expand the scope of government a lot more.

CIVIL LIBERTIES

"Which of the following comes closest to your opinion on the conflicting demands of national security and civil liberties?"

We have gone too far in the direction of national security, and have weakened our civil liberties.

We have struck a pretty good balance between the conflicting demands of national security and civil liberties.

We have gone too far in the direction of preserving civil liberties, and
have weakened our national security.

Apparently these are not burning issues which split the respondents into
hostile camps, for in both cases the largest group of participants managed
to light between the horns of the dilemma.

Now, let us look at the cross-tabulation of the two items.

TABLE 62

Government and Civil Liberties

Per cent of total sample

Civil Liberties	Government			Total
	Need to Cut Back	Neutral	Need to Expand	
Too much security	12 (201)	26 (451)	4 (68)	42
Neutral	13 (217)	35 (599)	1 (24)	49
Too much civil liberties	2 (41)	7 (113)	* (13)	9
	27%	68%	5%	100%

(Base N in parentheses)

* Less than one per cent.

One of the interesting things about Table 62 is that there is not much
correlation between the two items.

While the small number of need-to-expanders do appear more worried
about threats to civil liberties, there is little or no difference in the civil-
liberties position of the two large groups — the neutrals and the need-to-
cut-backers.

Perhaps the best way to think of Table 62 is in terms of a map of the
political terrain. In the center we find the area of the "Contented," those
participants who are happy with the current state of affairs with regard to
both governmental activities and civil liberties. Moving away from this
center, up in the northeast corner of Table 62 ("Need to Expand" and
"Too Much Security") we come to the territory of the New Deal Demo-
crat. In the opposite direction, down in the southwest territory, lies the
domain of the arch-conservative, the classical Midwest Republican, and
some Texas Democrats. Moving across to the southeast corner, we find a
combination which is rare in American politics, thirteen respondents whose
answers, if taken literally, imply a totalitarian ideology. Finally, up in the
northwest quadrant, we find what might have been thought of as an ex-
tinct species but is actually the most common of the extreme types, the
combination of "Need to Cut Back" and "Too Much Security." This has
the distinct air of 18th century liberalism.

We should stress that the labels we have given to these combinations
are descriptive, not analytical, in the sense that we are not implying that

these positions can be traced in any causal sense to the historic ideologies which provided the names. Rather, we have used these labels to convey the "feel" of the combination of values represented. In an informal communication, Professor Peter Rossi of the University of Chicago has informed us that the position we call "18th century liberalism" has been found, in a number of unpublished studies, to be common among high-status professionals. Perhaps we should call it "the new conservatism," but since the term we picked has a sort of Great Bookish ring to it, we will stick to it.

Following this analogy, we divided the respondents as follows (excluding the "totalitarians" because there were only thirteen of them):

TABLE 63

Ideological Types

Type and Government	Civil Liberties		Per cent
18th Century Liberals:			*51*
Cut back	Too much security	12	
Cut back	Neutral	13	
Neutral	Too much security	26	
Contenteds:			*35*
Neutral	Neutral	35	
Arch-conservatives:			*9*
Cut back	Too much civil liberties	2	
Neutral	Too much civil liberties	7	
New Dealers:			*5*
Expand	Too much security	4	
Expand	Neutral	1	

Obviously, the combinations are arbitrary, and the absolute proportions could be varied considerably by re-assigning the mixed categories. We chose the path we did, however, through our terrain (or possibly jungle) for the plain and simple reason that it appears that the tendency of Great Book is to increase the proportion of 18th century liberals.

TABLE 64

Exposure and Political Ideology, Controlling for Drop-Outs
Per cent "18th Century Liberals"

1957 Exposure (years)	1958 Status		
	Dropped	Continued	Total
3+	64 (77)	59 (303)	60 (380)
1 and 2	39 (122)	53 (371)	49 (493)
0	45 (258)	48 (320)	47 (578)
	(Base N in parentheses)		

The cross-sectional comparison in the Total column suggests an increase in 18th century liberalism, and our two control comparisons, indicated by the arrows, substantiate the conclusion that in the advanced years, at least, these differences are not due to drop-outs (for the advanced-year comparison, p <.05).

Other tables, which we shall not reprint here, indicate that the proportion of "passives" declines, but not the proportion of Conservatives and New Dealers. This suggests that the change tends to come from "selling" the passives, not proselytizing the Conservatives and New Dealers.

COMMUNITY INVOLVEMENT

This chapter deals with the involvement of Great Books members in the civic and organizational life of their communities. The general question is whether association with the program has any effect on involvement in the community.

Involvement is looked at in two ways: interest in public affairs, and membership in voluntary associations or informal groups dealing with community problems.

Since there is no evidence that the program attracted different sorts of people last year from those to whom it appealed in the few years preceding, last year's beginners probably provide a good picture of the people who enter the Great Books program. Any consideration of their involvement in their communities must start from the fact that most of them have the sort of educational and occupational background which tends to be associated with membership in voluntary associations.

A recent summary of survey findings on the voluntary association memberships of American adults [1] provides a base against which Great Books participants can be compared.

TABLE 65

Membership in Organizations by Formal Education:
Great Books Entrants and a U.S. National Sample†
Per cent with membership in organization

	Education					
	12 Years		Some College		College Degree or More	
Number of Organizations	Great Books*	U.S.	Great Books	U.S.	Great Books	U.S.
0	37	57	35	46	32	20
1	33	23	28	24	23	30
2 and more	30	20	37	30	45	36
N=	(119)	(610)	(169)	(232)	(416)	(170)

† National sample figures taken from Table 3 of the Wright and Hyman article.
*Includes entrants with less than four years of high school.

A look at Table 65 indicates that participants are somewhat more involved in organizations than are other Americans of comparable education. The entrants who have not attended college have a strikingly lower

[1] Charles R. Wright and Herbert H. Hyman, "Voluntary Association Membership of American Adults: Evidence from National Sample Surveys." *American Sociological Review,* June, 1958, Vol. 23, No. 3, pp. 284-294.

percentage of people who do not belong to any organizations and a higher percentage of people who belong to two or more; the part-college entrants show the same differences, although in lesser degree; the college graduates have a higher percentage of people who do not belong to any organization but balance it by also having a higher percentage who belong to two or more organizations. We excluded from the tally membership in churches, organizations attached to particular congregations, and adult education programs. Had we included them, all categories of Great Books participants would almost certainly have shown more memberships than the people in the national sample.

Since the basic question of this section is the community involvement of Great Books participants, we need some way of describing people on the basis of the pattern of their public-affairs interests and organizational activities. With such a description in hand, we can then relate a number of attributes to some other factor simultaneously rather than having to analyze each relationship in turn.

The first question then becomes whether people have patterns in their interests and organizational activities. The answer is that they do.

Patterns of Interest in Public Affairs

The questionnaire asked about interest in local politics, civic organizations, national politics, and gave choices of answers ranging from definite lack of interest to high interest in each of these areas.[2]

Table 66, below, measures the association between high interest in any one of the areas and in each of the others.

The general meaning of the table, and of the individual tables from which the Q's were derived, is that there are definite patterns in areas of interests. People who say that they are highly interested in either world affairs or national politics in the great majority of cases also say that they are highly interested in the other. Similarly, people who are highly interested in civic organizations are usually interested in local politics, and people highly interested in local politics tend to be highly interested in civic organizations. There is also something of a political axis of interest: people highly interested in local politics tend to be highly interested in national politics and the reverse. However, this relationship is lower than the others. The more striking finding is that the participants' interests split into two geographical areas, local and what may be called the cosmopolitan. (We should stress that this use of the term is different from its use in Part B.)

---

[2] Throughout the analysis "highly interested" equals "replied that they are 'very interested' " in whatever matter is under consideration. "Rise in high interest" and similar phrases mean that the percentage of respondents saying that they are "very interested" rises.

TABLE 66

Relationships Among High Interest in Public Areas: Values of Q

Public affairs areas	Local politics	Civic organizations	National politics	World affairs
Local politics	—	.732	.659	.336
Civic organizations	.732	—	.397	.202
National politics	.659	.397	—	.925
World affairs	.336	.202	.925	—

In the course of a study of personal influence in a town on the eastern seaboard, Professor Robert Merton of Columbia University developed the distinction between types of influential people: the local and the cosmopolitan.[4] The distinction does not refer to the area in which influence was exerted; in both cases the influence was personal and was limited to the local area. The distinction lay in the orientation to the town; for Merton's "locals," the town was the world, while for the "cosmopolitans," the town, while a pleasant place to live, was one among many.

Merton's analysis suggests that people tend to be *either* locals or cosmopolitans. Our interest materials, however, have a different pattern. These data, like the musical sophistication items discussed in the previous chapter, show the step pattern of the Guttman scale. That is, our locals tended to be interested in everything the cosmopolitans were interested in, *plus* local politics or civic organizations. Putting it another way, interest in world and national affairs appears to be a *necessary*, although not *sufficient*, condition for interest in local affairs in this population. Thus, while it is true that only 27 per cent of those interested in world affairs were also interested in local politics, among those not highly interested in world affairs, only 13 per cent were interested in local politics. Table 67 shows the Guttman scale pattern for world affairs, national politics, and local politics.

TABLE 67

Guttman Scale of Areas of High Interest:
Local Politics — National Politics — World Affairs

Local Politics	National Politics	World Affairs	N
+	+	+	297
−	+	+	620
−	−	+	239
−	−	−	441
			1,597
	Error Types		
−	+	−	36
+	−	−	50
+	+	−	32
+	−	+	20
	R = .97		138

[4] Robert K. Merton, "Patterns of Influence: Local and Cosmopolitan Influentials," in Robert K. Merton, *Social Theory and Social Structure* (rev. ed.), (Glencoe, Ill.: Free Fress, 1957), pp. 387-420.

Not all the Great Books participants can be classified as "local" or "non-local" in their areas of high interest; some have no area of public affairs in which they are highly interested. They may be "fairly interested" in several areas, of course, and many of them are. However, they are people who did not feel great enough interest to put themselves in the top category of even one of the four areas offered. In this they differ from the 77 per cent of the participants who have at least one area of high interest in public affairs. Table 68 below shows the distribution of participants in terms of interest areas.

TABLE 68

Per Cent Distribution of Respondents by Areas of High Interest

Local		31
Local only	5*	
Local and Nonlocal	26	
Nonlocal (National-World)		46
No Area of High Interest		23

(N=1,847)

* The local-nonlocal division fails to mark off the 92 people with purely local interests from their 480 fellow "locals" who also have broader interests, but this makes fewer difficulties than a subcategory of only 92 cases would. The "pure locals" are so small a proportion of the "locals" that they cannot usually have any important influence on findings concerning the "local" group as a whole.

So far, then, we have a division of people on the basis of their areas of high interest (or lack of them) in public affairs.

Participation Patterns in Voluntary and Other Local Groups

On the basis of both common experience and studies of the organizational participation of Americans, it seemed sensible to assume that Great Books participants would differ in their organizational "activeness" as well as in the nature and extent of their interests. On this assumption it seemed reasonable to divide people *within* each area of interest into those who were relatively active and whose who were relatively inactive in terms of organizational participation. After both substantive and statistical consideration, it was decided to use membership in at least two organizations as the criterion for being "active."[4]

Among the "active" people, it seems reasonable to make some distinctions based on the kinds of organizations to which they belong and the amount of responsibility they have carried. Especially among people with high local interest, two subtypes of "activeness" turned up often enough to justify a separate category of "AAA Active" locally interested people. They were holding local office and carrying major responsibility in private organizations working for the melioration of some community problem.

---

[4] People who failed to answer the question on their organizational memberships were put in the "inactive" category. This was done because the unusually high proportion of failures to answer the question on organizations combined with low nonresponse rates on the surrounding questions suggested that leaving the question blank had often been intended to indicate that the respondent did not belong to any organizations.

Among people carrying less responsibility than these, there still seemed to be a logical division based on the nature of the organization to which they belonged. Membership in purely social organizations, in professional organizations, or in organizations based on some special interest or social characteristic may reflect a different sort of relationship to one's community from membership in organizations of a "Red Feather" sort or in organizations concerned with policies and problems of the community as a whole. The last, whether political "action" organizations such as the county Republican Committee, or nonpartisan civic action organizations such as Better Government Associations, seemed logically to represent a special sort of involvement in one's community and were used as the basis of a category of activeness. (Partly because of the problem of sampling error when numbers in categories get small, and partly because most of the people belonging to a "Red Feather" organization also belong to an "action" organization, membership in "Red Feather" organizations was not used as the basis of a separate category.)

Out of all the considerations above came nine categories of a typology, the three categories of interest and divisions of activeness within each category of interest.

THE INTEREST-ACTIVITY TYPOLOGY

N

A. Local: expresses high interest in either or both local politics and civic organizations

  AAA Active: holds or has held local office or has organized a group to take action about one or more community problems or has been a major office holder in an established organization taking action about one or more local problems   116

  AA Active: is a member of two or more organizations at least one of which is an "action" organization or has taken nonleadership group action about one or more local problems   267

  A Active: is a member of two or more organizations neither of which is an "action" organization   54

  Inactive: belongs to fewer than two organizations and has not participated in any group activity about a local problem   137

B. Nonlocal: expresses high interest in either world affairs or national politics, or both, but does not express high interest in either local politics or civic organizations

AA Active:	belongs to two or more organizations of which at least one is an "action" organization	125
A Active:	belongs to two or more organizations of which neither is an "action" organization	192
Inactive:	belongs to fewer than two organizations	534
C. No High Interest:	does not express high interest in local politics or civic organizations or national politics or world affairs	
A Active:	belongs to two or more organizations (of any kind)	153
Inactive:	belongs to fewer than two organizations	271
Not classifiable	. . . .	60
		1,909

Now, let us consider the question of whether continued participation in Great Books leads to changes in community involvement. Unlike our purely intellectual measures, we have no clear-cut expected direction of change. It could be that the program tends to draw people away from community involvement because it heavily involves them in the program itself. It could also be that the program does effect changes, but that they reinforce the global interests of the members we have already noted, rather than the local involvement. Finally, it could be that contact and discussion with others living in the same community could lead to greater involvement in local affairs.

To begin with subjective materials, it is clear that the members of the sampled groups believe that their readings are relevant to local community affairs, and also that this belief increases with continued participation in Great Books. In our questionnaire we asked the participants to list what they believed to be the most important current problems in their local community. Then we asked them whether "your participation in Great Books has affected your understanding of the problem or your activity regarding the problem."

TABLE 69

Exposure and Reported Relevance of Great Books to Community Problems, Controlling for Drop-Out

Per cent reporting some effect

1957 Exposure (years)	1958 Status		
	Dropped	Continued	Total
3+	53 (49)	65 (215)	63 (264)
1 and 2	41 (68)	56 (245)	53 (313)
0	30 (159)	37 (213)	34 (372)

(Base N in parentheses)

The trend comparisons (both highly significant statistically) are among the strongest we have seen in the follow-up data. Clearly, regardless of the community problem reported, and regardless of the specific effect reported, Great Books members increasingly come to see the program has relevance to specific local problems. This is not the whole story, however, for not many of these effects were reported as galvanic impulses to do something about the problem; rather, the respondents usually reported increased intellectual understanding of the problem. In a separate part of the schedule we asked, "With regard to solving specific social and community problems . . ." do the Great Books (a) "provide both an understanding of the problems and a key to plans of action," (b) "provide an intellectual understanding of the problems, but few or no keys to plans of action," or (c) "are they not applicable to specific social and community problems"? While less than 15 per cent picked (c), only about one-quarter picked (a), the bulk claiming relevance but denying specific implications for social action.

When, then, we turn to our index of activity and interest, what do we find? We shall not reproduce the drop-out controls here, since the index is so complex that it requires several tables to present the full picture. Rather, if we may be trusted, we will summarize the findings:

(1) The proportion who are active in some local organization does rise in both of the key comparisons, but the differences are not within the conventional limits of statistical significance (p $<.10$).

(2) The proportion with no area of high interest also shows a slight trend toward decline, but the statistical reliability of the trends is negligible.

(3) There appears to be no trend at all toward either more local or less local orientation among those who do report some area of interest.

These conclusions can, however, be read two ways. The person who believes that Great Books is an effective vehicle for involving educated people in other community affairs finds little support in terms of concrete changes of orientation or civic activities, although on the purely intellectual level a strong effect occurs. Conversely, however, the person who believes that Great Books is a retreatist organization which draws its members away from Athens, Ohio or Athens, Georgia and toward Athens, Greece, can find little comfort in our data, for the members are already rather active in their communities, and what trends we find suggest increases rather than decreases.

Summary

In this chapter we have examined changes in values, ideologies, and community involvement. Our general question was that of assessing the carry-over from Great Books to the members' orientations and involvement in the community and society. In general, we found no evidence that Great Books can be thought of as a process of indoctrination, but certain definite trends did appear in our data.

We found no evidence that the members change in their basic values, in the priority they give to such large-scale abstractions as hedonism, contemplation, group affiliation, or tangible activity.

At the level of specific ideological positions, however, we think we did spot some directions of change. Continued exposure to Great Books does seem to affect intellectual orientations toward religions and also seems to lead to change in certain political positions. The religious trends appear to be in the direction of greater acceptance of liberal and skeptical approaches to religion, without, however, abandonment of prior religious faith. The political trend is toward "18th century liberalism," (or perhaps new conservativism) defined as increased concern about civil liberties combined with opposition to government controls in other areas.

Involvement in the local community shows little change. The members come to the program highly involved, although typically more interested in the larger national or world scene than in the local milieu. Exposure to Great Books does seem to the members themselves to affect their understanding of local issues or problems, but in terms of indices of interest and activity, no strong trends were found.

Summary

SUMMARY

The following paragraphs summarize the major findings of our survey of the Great Books program. In the report itself, these conclusions are developed from rather extensive statistical analysis and are subject to a number of qualifications and specifications which we have left out of the summary. We hope that any reader who wishes to make serious use of these findings will avail himself of the full text in addition to this brief over-view.

What Are the Participants Like?

In a capsule, Great Books participants tend to be well-educated, high-status, socially active, youngish adults.

It is perhaps more interesting to note what they are not. They are not "ivory-tower intellectuals," but rather show "middlebrow" intellectual interests; and far from being alienated from their society, they share its middle-class values and norms of community participation. Neither are they "social misfits," for the old and the unmarried (people for whom society often has no niche) are under-represented; and for most of the members, Great Books is only one among a fairly large number of formal and informal social groups to which they belong. The "climber," while not unrepresented in the program, is not a frequent type; if anything, the members are already more highly educated and less upwardly mobile socially than comparable adults.

What Do They Want from the Program?

Great Books attracts people with a wide diversity of motivations, from those who want to learn speed-reading to those who want to solve the world's problems. Most of the members come with a varied collection of aims, some of which are abstractly intellectual and a lot of which are highly pragmatic. The discussion group itself appears to be important, for we found many members reporting a cluster of motives which indicated they were concerned about the intellectual narrowness of their lives and wanted not just knowledge of great authors but also contact with other group members who shared their intellectual orientations. It is the combination of the social and the intellectual — not one or the other — which appears to be the hallmark of the participants' motivations.

What Do They Say They Get from the Program?

Levels of satisfaction run high, partly because the dissatisfied quickly drop out of the program. Large proportions of those who continue reported that participation in Great Books has had a "genuine impact" on their lives, high impact being more common among those who started from a lower level of cultural sophistication. Specific "effects" vary considerably in their reported attainment, and two things seem to relate to differences in the effectiveness of different program aims. First, it is always the case that people who wanted a specific effect are more likely to report achieving it. Great Books is apparently diffuse enough so that the major determinant of an effect is the participant's motivations. Beyond this, we noted that those things which "pay off" right in the discussion groups (e.g., "getting a chance to express ideas I had been thinking and reading about") seemed much more effective than those things which required applications to the resistant world outside the immediate program (e.g., "finding solutions to contemporary social problems").

Special Effects
Knowledge

The strongest and clearest effect of continued participation in Great Books is increased knowledge of the liberal arts and humanities. Even when a number of statistical controls are applied, the advanced year participant is considerably more knowledgeable than the first year participant. After three years or more in the program the participant with no college training scores about as well on the knowledge test as the beginning member who has a bachelor's degree.

Esthetics

The respondents were given a test of their ability to judge excellence in verse and a measure of their familiarity with classical music. It was our conclusion that in neither case could we show that the program has any effect in these esthetic areas, advanced-year members being no better judges of these matters than beginners. Since the program excludes music, there is no reason why musical tastes should improve; but the members do read a considerable amount of verse, apparently without gains in general poetic sensitivity.

Reading

The Great Books participants are heavy readers, and apparently read more than people of comparable education, even aside from preparation for the discussions. Their non-program reading is considerably less challenging than the curriculum of the program, and runs, metaphorically speaking, somewhere between the Book of the Month Club and Book Find Club. Continued participation in the program does seem to increase the number of hours spent both in "serious" reading and in preparation for the discussions, although our measures of "quality" failed to detect a trend in level of difficulty of outside readings.

Values and Ideologies

The advanced-year participant has not only learned more about the content of Great Books, but is also quite likely to report that he has been persuaded by them and has changed his mind on the value of some author or school of thought. Our survey was unable to detect any changes in basic values for the participant, but we did find evidence of some shifts in religious and political positions. In general, members of each major faith show a less single-minded dedication to their own denominational position and a greater acceptance of "liberal" alternatives. The trend is not interpreted as one of dramatic changes in faith but rather as an expansion of the breadth and scope of religious ideas which are considered to be worth serious attention. Political changes appear to be more clear-cut, the trend being for an increase in concern about loss of civil liberties, accompanied by an increase in concern about too much government — a syndrome which may be alternatively interpreted as "18th century liberalism" or "new conservativism."

Community Involvement

We divided community involvement into two aspects, expressed interest in local and civic affairs, and overt activity in community organizations and events. It turns out that different things happen in these two areas of involvement.

In terms of interest, we find that the participants are quite interested in the local scene and in civic affairs but that, relatively speaking, they show greater interest in the national and world arenas than they do in their home towns. Exposure to the program doesn't seem to alter this picture toward either increased or decreased localism.

In terms of activities, we find that the participants are quite active in terms of memberships in organizations and participation in programs to change or improve the community. Activity may increase with exposure to Great Books, although our findings are not strong enough to be statistically reliable.

If, however, we limit our consideration to intellectual awareness of local community affairs instead of overt action to do something about them, we do find a strong trend. There appears to be a steady increase in the proportion of members who report that the Great Books have a distinct relevance for the understanding of specific problems in their local community.

Any attempt to achieve a final balancing of the books here is beyond the commission of the researcher, for it requires decisions about the relative weight of the high success areas — increased knowledge, changes in ideologies, and participants' subjective satisfactions; the areas of smaller change, such as reading and community activity; and the areas of no effect at all, esthetics and basic values. In addition, even if such a balance could be determined, we would have no idea whether another program or a modified version of the current program would do as well, or better. Such final conclusions will have to be drawn by the reader on the basis of his own system of values and his evaluation of the practical possibilities in the world of adult education in the liberal arts and humanities.

Appendices

Appendix I

THE GREAT BOOKS READINGS

First Year:
Declaration of Independence
Plato: *Apology; Crito*
Sophocles: *Antigone*
Aristotle: *Politics,* Bk. I
Plutarch: *Lycurgus & Numa,* with a comparison
The Gospel according to St. Matthew
Epictetus: *Discourses,* Bk. I, Chs. 1-4, 6, 9, 11, 15, 17, 20, 23, 26;
    Bk. II, Ch. 8
Machiavelli: *The Prince*
Shakespeare: *Macbeth*
Milton: *Areopagitica*
Adam Smith: *The Wealth of Nations,* Bk. I, Chs. 1-9, 11; Bk. IV, parts
The Federalist, Nos. 1, 10, 15, 51; *Constitution of the United States*
De Tocqueville: *Democracy in America,* Vol. II, Bk. I, Chs. 1-4; Bk. II,
    Chs. 1, 2, 4-15, 19, 20; Bk. IV

Marx & Engels: *The Communist Manifesto*
Thoreau: *On Civil Disobedience; Walden*, Chs. 1, 2, 11, 17, 18
Tolstoy: *The Death of Ivan Ilyitch*
A Great Books Primer

Second Year:
   Ecclesiastes
   Homer: *The Odyssey*
   Sophocles: *Oedipus Rex; Oedipus at Colonus*
   Plato: *Meno*
   Aristotle: *Ethics*, Bks. I; X, Chs. 6-9
   Lucretius: *Of the Nature of Things*, Bks. I-III
   St. Augustine: *Confessions*, Bks. I-VIII
   Shakespeare: *Hamlet*
   Descartes: *Discourse on Method*
   Hobbes: *Leviathan*, Intro.; Pt. I, Chs. 11-16, Pt. II, Chs. 17, 18, 29
   Pascal: *Pensées*, selections
   Swift: *Gulliver's Travels*
   Rousseau: *On the Origin of Inequality*
   Kant: *Perpetual Peace*
   Mill: *On Liberty*
   Mark Twain: *The Adventures of Huckleberry Finn*
   A Great Books Reader

Third Year:
   The Book of Job
   Aeschylus: *The Oresteia*, a trilogy
   Thucydides: *History of the Peloponnesian War*, Bk. I, Chs. 1, 3, 5-7;
      Bk. V, Ch. 17
   Plato: *Symposium*
   Aristotle: *Politics*, Bks. III-V
   St. Thomas Aquinas: *Treatise on Law:* QQ. 90-97 from the *Summa
      Theologica*, I-II
   Rabelais: *Gargantua & Pantagruel*, Bk. I
   Calvin: *Institutes*, Bk. II, Ch. 2; Bk. IV, Ch. 20
   Shakespeare: *King Lear*
   Francis Bacon: *Novum Organum*, Bk. I
   Locke: *Of Civil Government*
   Voltaire: *Candide*
   Rousseau: *The Social Contract*, Bks. I-II
   Gibbon: *The Decline and Fall of the Roman Empire*, Chs. 15, 16
   Dostoyevsky: *The Brothers Karamazov*, Pt. II, Bk. V, Ch. 5; Bk. VI,
      Chs. 1-3

Freud: *The Origin & Development of Psychoanalysis*
A Great Books Reader II

Fourth Year:
Confucius: *The Analects*, selections
Plato: *The Republic*, Bks. VI-VII
Aristophanes: *Lysistrata; The Clouds*
Aristotle: *Poetics*
Euclid: *Elements of Geometry*, Bk. I
Marcus Aurelius: *Meditations*
Sextus Empiricus: *Outlines of Pyrrhonism*, Bk. I
Song of the Volsungs and the Nibelungs
St. Thomas Aquinas: *On Truth and Falsity:* QQ. 16-17 from the
    Summa Theologica, I
Montaigne: *Essays*, Bk. I, Chs. XL, XXII, XXIV, XXVI, XXX
Shakespeare: *The Tempest*
Locke: *An Essay Concerning Human Understanding*, Bk. III, Chs. I,
    III, IX-XI
Milton: *Paradise Lost*
Hume: *An Enquiry Concerning Human Understanding*
Nietzsche: *Beyond Good and Evil*, Chs. I, III, V, VI, VII, IX
William James: *Pragmatism*, selections

Fifth Year:
Euripides: *Medea, Hippolytus, Trojan Women*
Plato: *Theaetetus*
Aristotle: *Physics*, Bk. IV, Chs. 1-4, 6-7, 10-13
Virgil: *Aeneid*
St. Francis: *Little Flowers*
St. Thomas Aquinas: *Treatise on Man:* QQ. 75-79 from the *Summa
    Theologica*, I
Dante: *Divine Comedy:* Hell, Purgatory
Dante: *Divine Comedy:* Paradise
Pico della Mirandola: *Oration on the Dignity of Man*
Berkeley: *Principles of Human Knowledge*
Newton: *Mathematical Principles of Natural Philosophy*, selections
Boswell: *Life of Johnson*, selections
Kant: *Prolegomena*
Woolman: *Journal*
Melville: *Moby Dick*
Einstein: *Relativity: The Special & General Theory*

Sixth Year:

Aeschylus: *Prometheus Bound*

Plato: *Phaedrus*

Aristotle: *Metaphysics,* Bk. XII

Longinus: *On the Sublime*

St. Augustine: *On Nature and Grace; On Grace and Free Will*

St. Thomas Aquinas: *The Existence and Simplicity of God:* QQ. 2-3 from the *Summa Theologica,* I

Chaucer: *Canterbury Tales,* selections

Shakespeare: *Richard II*

Cervantes: *Don Quixote,* Pt. I

Spinoza: *Ethics,* Pt. I

Hume: *Dialogues Concerning Natural Religion*

Voltaire: *Philosophical Dictionary,* selections

Hegel: *Philosophy of History,* Intro. and Classification of Historic Data

Darwin: *The Origin of Species,* Chs. I-VI, XV

Melville: *Billy Budd, Foretopman*

Henry James: *The Turn of the Screw*

Appendix II
THE QUESTIONNAIRE

NATIONAL OPINION RESEARCH CENTER

University of Chicago

Survey 408

11/57

1. When did you attend your first Great Books Discussion group meeting?

    Fall 1957.........

    "   1956.........

    "   1955.........

    "   1954.........

    Other.............

2. Have you been with this group continuously since you began Great Books?

    Yes....... *No.......

    *IF "NO": Did you attend another group meeting, or drop out of the program temporarily, or what?

3. How many meetings of this group have you attended, since it started this Fall? (If your group docsn't start in the Fall, please tell us the number of meetings you have attended since September 1.)

4. Have you ever "led" a Great Books Discussion? *Yes_____1 No_____2
   IF "YES":
   1._____I am the current leader or co-leader of this group.
   2._____I am one of the current rotating leaders of this group.
   3._____I have been the leader or co-leader of this group, but am not leading now.
   4._____I have been the leader or co-leader of another group, but am not leading now.
   5._____I am the current leader or co-leader of another group, but attend this one as a participant.
   6._____Other_____

5. Have you ever had a Great Books Leader Training Course?
   Yes_____ No_____

6. How would you rate your attendance in this group?
   1._____I attend every meeting
   2._____I attend all but a few meetings
   3._____I attend most meetings
   4._____I attend some meetings, but not most
   5._____I attend on occasion
   6._____This is my first meeting with this group, so I can't say

Listed below are 23 "results" of participating in Great Books.

1. Please think back to the time when you decided to attend your first Great Books meeting.

   In the *left hand column* please check any item on the list which you definitely had in mind as a reason for joining — regardless of whether or not Great Books met this expectation.

2. In the *right hand column,* please place a check by any of the items which you think has definitely been an effect of Great Books for you — regardless of whether or not it was a reason for joining.

Reason for Joining		Effect of Great Books
	1. Improving my reading skills.	
	2. Making new friends.	
	3. Improving my taste in fiction and poetry.	
	4. Escaping the intellectual narrowness of my occupation.	
	5. Becoming more sure of myself when talking with people of higher educational background.	

Reason for Joining		Effect of Great Books
	6. Developing the ability to lead group discussions outside of Great Books.	
	7. Escaping the intellectual narrowness of my community.	
	8. Gaining insight into myself and my personal problems.	
	9. Improving my ability to carry out my job through the intellectual training of reading Great Books.	
	10. Gaining the equivalent of a college education.	
	11. Developing common interests with my spouse.	
	12. Gaining a better intellectual background for my participation in community organizations and community affairs.	
	13. Escaping the intellectual narrowness of being a housewife.	
	14. To learn what the greatest minds in history have to say about the basic issues of life.	
	15. Getting a chance to express ideas I had been thinking and reading about.	
	16. Reacquainting myself with a cultural background which had become rusty.	
	17. Finding solutions to contemporary social problems.	
	18. Increasing my ability to carry out my job through improving my ability to participate in group discussions.	
	19. Supplementing an unduly narrow or technical college training.	
	20. Becoming a more effective participant in group discussions outside of Great Books.	
	21. Meeting people who are quite different from me.	
	22. Talking with people who have more intellectual interests than my usual "social" friends.	

Reason for Joining		Effect of Great Books
	23. Improving my ability to analyze and criticize arguments.	
	24. Other --	
	--	
	--	
	--	

1. Since you began Great Books have there been any particular authors or schools of thought which you once disliked, but now find more acceptable?

*Yes_____1   No_____2

IF "YES": Which ones?

Why was there a change?

2. Since you began Great Books are there any particular authors or schools of thought which you once accepted, but now find less acceptable?

*Yes_____1   No_____2

IF "YES": Which ones?

Why was there a change?

READING

1. On the average, about how many hours per week do you spend on the following types of reading?
   1) For relaxation (detective stories, light fiction, sports section of the newspaper, etc.)   ----------
   2) Preparation for Great Books discussion groups   ----------
   3) Serious reading on your own (history, philosophy, serious novels, etc., not connected with Great Books or with your job)   ----------

2. Since you began Great Books, has the amount of time spent on the following changed?

	5	4	3	2	1
	Increased a Lot	Increased a Little	No Change	Decreased a Little	Decreased a Lot
1) Reading for relaxation.					
2) Preparation for Great Books.					
3) Serious reading on your own.					

3. Hours of reading aside, do you think Great Books has had any effect on your reading — aside from preparing for the discussions?

4. Do you own a set of the Great Books readings which your group is discussing this year?

> 0........No
>
> 1........No, but I intend to purchase them
>
> 2........Yes

5. What book or books — outside of the Great Books readings — which you read in the last year impressed you as particularly worthwhile?

6. Following is a list of magazines. Please check each in the appropriate column.

	5	4	3	2	1
	I read it regularly	I read it on occasion but not regularly	I have seen a copy now and then, but I seldom read it	I've heard about it but I've never seen a copy of it	Never heard of this one
1) Art News					
2) The Gadfly					
3) Harper's					
4) High Fidelity					
5) New Republic					
6) New Yorker					
7) Partisan Review					
8) Reader's Digest					
9) Saturday Evening Post					
10) Saturday Review					
11) Scientific American					
12) Time					

WAYS TO LIVE

Below are listed four ways to live which various persons at various times have advocated and followed.

Indicate by numbers in the spaces below each "way to live" how much you, yourself, like or dislike each of them, using the following scale:

> 7 . . I like it very much
>
> 6 . . I like it quite a lot
>
> 5 . . I like it slightly

4 . . I am indifferent to it
3 . . I dislike it slightly
2 . . I dislike it quite a lot
1 . . I dislike it very much

Rate each one in terms of the *kind of life you personally would like to live*, not in terms of the kind of life you now lead, the kind of life you think is prudent to live in our society, or the kind you think is good for other people.

(1)

Life is something to be enjoyed — sensuously enjoyed, enjoyed with relish and abandonment. The aim in life should not be to control the course of the world or society or the lives of others, but to be open and receptive to things and persons, and to delight in them. To let oneself go, to let things and persons affect oneself, is more important than to "do" — or to "do good."

RATING OF #1_____

(2)

A person should merge oneself with a social group, enjoy cooperation and companionship, join with others in resolute activity for the realization of common goals. Persons are social and persons are active; life should merge energetic group activity and cooperative group enjoyment.

RATING OF #2_____

(3)

A person must stress the need of constant activity — physical action, adventure, the realistic solution of specific problems as they appear, the improvement of techniques for controlling the world and society. Man's future depends primarily on what he does, not on what he feels or on his speculations. Improvements must always be made if man is to progress. We can't just follow the past or dream of what the future might be.

RATING OF #3_____

(4)

The contemplative life is the good life. The external world is no fit habitat for man. It is too big, too cold, too pressing. Rather it is the life turned inward that is rewarding. The rich internal world of ideals, of sensitive feelings, of reverie, of self-knowledge is man's true home.

RATING OF #4_____

POETRY

Listed below and on the following pages are four poems. For each, three versions are given. Please check the version which you prefer as poetry.

Poem 1

A.   Tender, tender Sea Shell,
    Wilt thou sing me, please,
    Of thy happy, happy home
    'Neath the tropic trees?
    Ah, the coral islands!
    Ah, the wondrous fish!
    For such a song I'd give thee, dear,
    Whate'er a Shell could wish.

B.   Sea Shell, please sing me a song
    Of ships and sailor-men;
    Of strange kinds of birds and trees
    On the Spanish Main:
    Of fish and seaweed in the sea,
    And whatever creature there may be, —
    Sea Shell, please sing me a song!

C.   Sea Shell, Sea Shell,
    Sing me a song, Oh please!
    A song of ships and sailor men,
    Of parrots and tropical trees.
    Of islands lost in the Spanish Main
    Which no man ever may find again,
    Of fishes and coral under the waves,
    And sea-horses stabled in great green caves —
    Sea Shell, Sea Shell
    Sing me a song, Oh please!

Poem 2

A.   Let there be Light, said God, and lo! the Light
    Sprung from Tithonus' bed in darksome gloom,
    Deck'd her fair form in garments rich and rare
    And scattered smiles along the mournful sky.
    Her chariot of the Sun not yet created,
    Upon a cloud the nymph ethereal rode,
    And when the cloud wept raindrops down, she flung
    Comforting rainbows from her shining tent.

B.   Let there be light, said God, and forthwith Light
    Ethereal, first of things, quintessence pure,
    Sprung from the Deep, and from her native east
    To journey through the airy gloom began,
    Spher'd in a radiant cloud, for yet the Sun
    Was not; she in a cloudy tabernacle
    Sojourn'd the while. God saw the Light was good.

C.   And God said, "Let Light be," and there was Light
    The first ethereal created thing
    To being sprang, and daily from the east
    Began to travel through the darksome air;
    Until the golden sun should be created
    She sojourn'd in a radiant, shining cloud.
    God look'd upon the Light and it was good.

Preference_____   Preference_____

Poem 3

A. This was the routine they learned
Always at night when they returned
To lamps unlighted and fires gone gray
When they had been away all day.
They learned to build the fire up quick
With half a split-up kindling stick —
And knowing how the cat delights
To sleep indoors by the fire of nights,
They learned to leave the house door wide
For fear they might leave her shut outside.

B. Always — I tell you this they learned —
Always at night when they returned
To the lonely house from far away
To lamps unlighted and fire gone gray,
They learned to rattle the lock and key
To give whatever might chance to be
Warning and time to be off in flight:
And preferring the out- to the in-door night,
They learned to leave the house-door wide,
Until they had lit the lamp inside.

C. Always their hearts would thrill with fear
When at dead of night they again drew near
To the dismal, lonely, dark abode
Where not a glimmer of lamp-light showed.
Trembling, they turned the lock and key
With pallid face and shaking knee.
There was nothing to cause their fright,
But they felt more safe in the out-door night!
So they left the house-door open wide,
And fell in a faint on the floor inside.

Preference_____

Poem 4

A. Who sends the fog
so still and gray?
I fondly ask.
And Echo answers,
"E'en the same all-seeing Eye
that sends the still, gray cat."

B. The Fog is like a maltese cat,
it is so gray and still,
and like a cat it creeps
about the city streets.
How gray it is! How cat-like!
Especially when it steals away,
Just like a cat.

C. The fog comes
on little cat feet.
It sits looking
over harbor and city
on silent haunches
and then moves on.

Preference_____

DISCUSSION METHOD

1. How often should an "ideal" Great Books discussion leader . . .
   (Check each one)

	5	4	3	2	1
	Always	Usually	Sometimes	Seldom	Never
1) Tactfully squelch over-talkative participants?					
2) Summarize the results of the discussion?					
3) Give a short lecture on the historical and bio-graphical background of the reading?					
4) Refrain from communi-cating, even indirectly, his own opinion?					
5) "Cross-examine" a par-ticipant to clarify the discussion?					

2. On the whole, which of the following best describes your group? (If you have several leaders during the course of the year, try to estimate on the basis of an "average.") (Check one)

   1_____The leader always dominates the discussion.
   2_____The leader tends to dominate the discussion.
   3_____There is an equal balance between the leader's talking and the group's talking.
   4_____The leader seldom talks, except for a few comments and questions.

3. Some people have suggested that it would be a good idea for more decisions in business, education, and community organizations to be made on the basis of informal discussions like Great Books. Which of the following best describes your opinion? (Check one)

   1_____The discussion technique should be extended radically in business, education, and community organizations.
   2_____The discussion technique should be extended somewhat in business, education, and community organizations.
   3_____The discussion technique should neither be extended nor lessened in business, education, and community organizations.
   4_____The discussion technique should be lessened in business, education, and community organizations.

MUSIC

Let's assume that you are going to a concert tomorrow evening, and the following musical works might be on the program.

FIRST: Rate each in terms of its familiarity, as follows:
1. Very familiar — I'd recognize it if I heard it, even if the title wasn't announced.
2. Familiar — I might not know the title just from hearing it played, but it's something I've heard before and know a little about.
3. Less familiar — I don't know much about this specific work, but I am relatively familiar with the composer and the general type of music he is known for.
4. Unfamiliar — as far as I know, I've never heard this work, and I know little or nothing about the composer.

THEN: Regardless of familiarity, rate each work in terms of how much you might enjoy hearing it, as follows:
A. I'd enjoying hearing it very much — it probably would be one of the high points of the concert.
B. I'd enjoy hearing it, but it probably *wouldn't* be one of the high points of the concert.
C. Frankly, I'd just as soon skip this one.
D. I don't know enough about it or the composer even to guess.

	Familiarity	Enjoyment
1) Concerto No. 2 in B Flat Major for Piano (Brahms)		
2) 1812 Overture (Tchaikovsky)		
3) Missa Papae Marcelli (Palestrina)		
4) Music for Strings, Percussion, and Celeste (Bartok)		
5) Nutcracker Suite (Tchaikovsky)		
6) Rhapsody in Blue (Gershwin)		
7) Symphony No. 7 (Beethoven)		
8) Symphony No. 1 (Brahms)		
9) Symphony No. 2 (Ives)		
10) Symphony No. 41 ("Jupiter") by Mozart		
11) Trio No. 7 in B Flat Major ("Archduke") by Beethoven		
12) Variations on a Theme by Diabelli (Beethoven)		
13) William Tell Overture (Rossini)		

GREAT BOOKS AND THE COMMUNITY

1. What is your present street address? Street_____
    City_____ State_____

2. How long have you lived in that city?_____

3. What is your emotional feeling about your community? (Check one)
    1_____I feel I'm a real member of the community. I'm a part of it,
    and it's a part of me.
    2_____I do like the community, but I don't feel that I'm really a
    part of it.
    3_____I rather dislike the community, and I definitely do not feel
    I'm a part of it.

4. *For towns of its size,* how does your community rate as a place to live
    (in terms of housing, schools, services, etc.)? (Check one)
    1_____Outstanding
    2_____Very good, but not outstanding
    3_____Average
    4_____Below average
    5_____Poor

5. *For towns of its size,* how does your community rate in terms of cul-
    tural resources (art galleries, music, libraries, theaters, colleges, etc.)?
    (Check one)
    1_____Outstanding
    2_____Very good, but not outstanding
    3_____Average
    4_____Below average
    5_____Poor

6. What would you say were the two or three most important problems
    facing your community today?
    1) _____
    2) _____
    3) _____

7. For each of the problems you listed above, indicate below any ways
    in which you personally have been involved in community action to
    help solve them (e.g., circulating petitions, serving on committees,
    talking with your friends, contributing money).
    Problem 1)
    Problem 2)
    Problem 3)

8. For each of the problems you listed in question 6, indicate below any
    ways in which you think your participation in Great Books has affected
    your understanding of the problem or your activity regarding the
    problem.

Problem 1)   2)   3)

9. How would you rate your interest in the following areas?

	4	3	2	1
	Very Interested	Fairly Interested	Not Too Interested	Disinterested
1) Local politics				
2) Civic organizations				
3) National politics				
4) World affairs				
5) Church activities				

10. Please list below any civic or professional organizations in your community to which you belong (e.g., PTA, Labor unions, Kiwanis, Bar Association).

     1) _____

     2) _____

     3) _____

11. Have you ever held an official office in your community (mayor, member of library board, member of a city commission, etc.)?

           *Yes_____ No_____

IF "YES": Please indicate the office and dates you served.

	Office	Dates
1)		
2)		
3)		

12. How do you lean in national politics? (Check one)

     1_____ I'm a Democrat.

     2_____ I usually lean toward the Democratic candidates.

     3 _____ I usually split my ballot 50-50.

     4_____ I usually lean toward the Republican candidates.

     5_____ I'm a Republican.

13. Do you know of any "continuing education" programs or classes available in your community?

           *Yes_____ No_____

IF "YES": Describe them briefly.

1)   2)   3)

14. Have you ever participated in any of the "continuing education" programs you listed above?

*Yes.......   No.......

IF "YES": Which program was that?

	Program	Date
1)		
2)		

15. About how many evenings per month (on the average) do you spend in informal visiting and entertaining?

----

16. What is your religious preference?

----

17. How often do you attend religious services?

1.......Regularly, almost without exception   4.......Seldom

2.......Fairly regularly   5.......Never

3.......Occasionally

18. Listed below are various areas of activity and interest. Please check each in terms of whether your interest and involvement has changed since you first began attending Great Books.

	5	4	3	2	1
	Much More Involved and Interested	Somewhat More Involved and Interested	No Change	Somewhat Less Involved and Interested	Much Less Involved and Interested
1) Civic organizations					
2) Community problems and issues					
3) Local politics					
4) National politics					
5) World affairs					
6) Continuing education other than Great Books					
7) Informal visiting					
8) Church attendance					

Each of the 32 drawings on this and the following pages should suggest something—some book, person, episode, or work of art. Please jot down next to each picture a word or phrase which identifies it. Guess if you are not certain. (The first answer has been given as an example.)

"*Sir Walter Raleigh spreading his cape for Queen Elizabeth*"

①

HISTORY AND POLITICS

②

③

④

⑤

⑥

⑦

LITERATURE

GROUP DISCUSSION

One of the most important aspects of Great Books is the process of group discussion. The questions in this and the following two pages will enable us to understand some of the ways in which different groups go about discussing the readings.

1. In many informal discussion groups a "division of labor" develops, so that some participants tend to specialize in certain aspects of the discussion process. Please check each of the "specialties" below in the appropriate column.

	I tend to specialize in this aspect.		
	3	2	1
	More than the other members of my group	About as often as the other members	Less often than the other members
a) Pulling the threads of the discussion together and getting different viewpoints reconciled.			
b) Joking and kidding, finding the potentially humorous implications of the discussion.			
c) Providing "fuel" for the discussion by introducing ideas and opinions for the rest of the group to discuss.			
d) Making tactful comments to heal any hurt feelings which might arise in the discussion.			
e) Clarification, getting the discussion to the point by getting terms defined and pointing out logical problems.			

2. The same "specialties" are repeated below. After each, jot down the names of any members of your group who tend to perform this role frequently.

a) Pulling the threads of the discussion together and getting different viewpoints reconciled.

1)--   2) --

b) Joking and kidding, finding the potentially humorous implications of the discussion.

1)..   2)..

c) Providing "fuel" for the discussion by introducing ideas and opinions for the rest of the group to discuss.

1)..   2)..

d) Making tactful comments to heal any hurt feelings which might arise in the discussion.

1)..   2)..

e) Clarification, getting the discussion to the point by getting terms defined and asking about logical problems.

1)..   2)..

3. How would you rate the "morale" of your group?

    1.......Extremely high   3.......Average

    2.......High   4.......Below average

        5.......Poor

4. How would you rate your group in terms of the members' interest in the program?

    1.......Almost all are very interested

    2.......Most are very interested

    3.......About half are very interested

    4.......A minority are very interested

    5.......Few or none are very interested

5. How would you rate the amount of agreement on ideas and issues in your group?

    1.......By-and-large, almost all of the members have pretty much the same views

    2.......By-and-large, most of the members have similar views, but there are a few who have very different points of view

    3.......By-and-large, the members differ greatly in their points of view on most issues

6. How would you rate the intellectual "calibre" of your group's discussions?

    1.......Almost all of the discussions are on a pretty serious intellectual level

    2.......Most of the discussions are on a pretty serious intellectual level, but some turn into sort of "bull sessions"

3......Most of the discussions are sort of "bull sessions," but
some are on a pretty serious intellectual level

4......Almost all of the discussions turn into "bull sessions"

7. How many of the members of your group (excluding your spouse) do
you see regularly outside of the group discussions?

OPINIONS

1. In general, which of the following statements comes closest to expressing your basic position on government in the United States?

1......There is too much government control today. Governmental
activities should be cut back.

2......There is a lot of government control today, but, in general,
it is called for by the needs of our society.

3   We need to expand the scope of government a lot more.

2. Which of the following comes closest to your opinion on the conflicting demands of national security and civil liberties?

1......We have gone too far in the direction of national security,
and have weakened our civil liberties.

2......We have struck a pretty good balance between the conflicting demands of national security and civil liberties.

3......We have gone too far in the direction of preserving civil
liberties, and have weakened our national security.

3. The course of history justifies . . . (Check one)

1......Optimism with respect to society's future.

2......Optimism with respect to society's future in some areas,
pessimism with respect to society's future in other areas.

3......Pessimism with respect to society's future.

4. The course of history is . . . (Check one)

1......Capricious

2......Purposive

3......Mechanistic

5. With regard to solving specific social and community problems . . .
(Check one)

1......The Great Books provide both an understanding of the problems and a key to plans of action.

2......The Great Books provide an intellectual understanding of the
problems, but few or no keys to plans of action.

3......The Great Books are not applicable to specific social and
community problems.

6. The universe is . . . (Check one)

    1____A society of selves.

    2____A set of material objects or energies.

    3____An intellectual system or structure.

7. Church-going aside, religious ideas and theological problems are . . . (Check one)

    1____Extremely important to me.

    2____Important to me, but not extremely so.

    3____A matter of relative indifference.

8. Below are 12 different systems of religious thought.

In the column headed "Most Congenial" please check the *three* systems which you find most congenial intellectually.

In the column headed "Least Congenial" please check the *three* systems which you find least congenial intellectually.

	Most Congenial	Least Congenial
Agnosticism		
Atheism		
Buddhism		
Christian Science		
"Fundamentalist" Protestantism		
"Liberal" Protestantism		
"Middle of the Road" Protestantism		
Mohammedanism		
Mysticism		
Orthodox Judaism		
Reform Judaism		
Thomism (Roman Catholicism)		

9. The moral person should . . . (Check one)

    1____Follow the established moral laws.

    2____Judge acts as right or wrong in terms of their consequences.

    3____Follow his personal conscience.

10. Suppose that you are a multi-millionaire philanthropist. The following programs have been submitted for your support. Please rank them

in terms of your preference. Place a "1" by the program you think is most worthy of your support, a "6" by the program you believe is least worthy of your support, etc.

------Publishing the works of young poets.

------Establishing a commission to implement improvements in urban problems like traffic, juvenile delinquency, and housing.

------Providing more counselors and psychologists for mental health work in the high schools.

------Fellowships for basic research in chemistry and physics.

------Raising the salaries of ministers.

------Providing free chamber music concerts.

11. Which of the following comes closest to the way you think about yourself?

      1------I don't like the phrase particularly, but I guess you'd have to call me an "intellectual."

      2------I consider myself an educated person, but not really an "intellectual."

      3------I haven't had too much education, so I can't really call myself either an "intellectual" or an "educated person," but I am pretty serious in my approach to things.

      4------I guess I'm sort of a "lowbrow" when it comes down to it.

EVALUATIONS

1. On the whole, which of the following best describes your feeling about Great Books?

      1------It is a marvelous program and has had a genuine impact on me

      2------It is a fine thing and I enjoy it very much, but I can't say it has changed me much

      3------I have enjoyed some parts of it, but on the whole I haven't gotten much out of it

      4------I haven't gotten anything at all out of Great Books

2. How do you feel about continuing in Great Books?

      1------I definitely plan to continue through the year and next year too, if the program is still available

      2------I definitely plan to continue through this year, but I'll have to wait and see about next year

      3------I may or may not continue through this year

      4------I probably won't continue until the end of the year

3. Even the most enthusiastic Great Books participant finds some things that cut down his interest in the program. Please check any of the fol-

lowing that might tend to decrease your interest in Great Books in the near future.

1.......My health
2.......Increased family responsibilities
3.......The program isn't sufficiently challenging intellectually
4.......My group is getting a little stale
5.......I want to get into other activities to apply the things I've gotten out of Great Books
6.......I've become interested in another continuing education program
7.......The time or place of the meeting is inconvenient for me
8.......I've gotten into other community activities which interest me more
9.......I'm cutting down on all of my outside activities
10.......I have to give more time and attention to my job
11.......I don't get much out of the readings
12.......Personality clashes in the group I'm in
13.......Great Books just isn't for me
14.......Other --

4. What would you think of these possible alternatives to Great Books, in comparison with your present set-up?

Keep your same discussion group, but: change the readings in the direction of more:	5 Definitely prefer the alternative	4 Probably prefer the alternative	3 "50-50"	2 Probably prefer the present arrangement	1 Definitely prefer the present arrangement
1) Fiction and poetry					
2) Science and math					
3) Current events					
4) Anthropology, psychology, sociology, economics, etc.					
5) Local community issues					
6) Religion					
7) Philosophy					
8) Fine arts					

9) The same content areas, but discuss the works of contemporary authors

---

Keep the same readings, but:
1) Join a different group

---

2) Take a course with a professionally trained teacher

---

3) Take a correspondence course

OTHER:

---

1. How old are you?

1......Under 25	5......40-44	9......60-64
2......25-29	6......45-49	0......65-69
3......30-34	7......50-54	X......70 and over
4......35-39	8......55-59	

2. Sex   1......Male   2......Female

3. Your full name*_____
   *Although you will not be identified in any way in the research report and your questionnaire will be treated as confidential, for the purposes of sampling, it is vitally important to have the name of every participant in the study.

4. Which of the following best describes your current situation?
   1......Housewife
   2......Employed full time
   3......Housewife with part time job
   4......Full time student
   5......Retired, not working at all
   6......Retired, working part time
   7......Other_____

5. What is the name and location of the last school you attended? (e.g., "McKinley High School, Smithville, Ohio" or "Wayne University, Detroit, Michigan")

   _____

6. Please check the highest grade you completed in school.
   1......Six grades or less
   2......Seventh grade through eleventh
   3......High school graduate
   4......Technical training beyond high school (e.g., business college)
   5......Some college, but no bachelor's degree

6____Bachelor's degree
7____Graduate work beyond the A.B., but no graduate degree
8____Master's degree
9____Doctor's degree
10____Other graduate degree (Please specify_____
_____)

7. What field did you specialize in in the last school you attended?
_____

8. IF YOU ARE CURRENTLY EMPLOYED:
   a) What is your occupation?_____
   b) What are the major duties of your job?
   _____
   c) What sort of organization do you work for (not the name, but the type, for instance, "a small factory" or "the public school system")?
   _____

9. Are you the chief wage earner of your family?   Yes____   *No____
   *IF "NO":
   a) Who is the chief wage earner?
             1____My husband
             2____My father
             3____Other _____
   b) Please describe the chief wage earner's job, as follows:
      Occupation _____
      Major duties of that job_____
      Type of organization_____

10. Were you born in the United States?   Yes____1 No____2

11. Were your parents born in the United States?
             1____Both born in U.S.
             2____One born in U.S.
             3____Neither born in U.S.

12. Were your grandparents born in the United States?
             1____All born in U.S.
             2____Some born in U.S., some not born in U.S.
             3____None born in U.S.

13. What is your "nationality background"?

14. What was your father's *usual* occupation? (Please describe it in some detail.)

    ----

15. Your marital status:
    1........Single (never married)
    2........Married, no previous marriage
    3........Married, a previous marriage
    4........Legally separated or divorced
    5........Widowed

Group Composition
and
Program Retention

A digest of Part I of a further analysis of the Great Books data by James A. Davis and his associates. The full text of this study is being published by The Free Press of Glencoe, Illinois, under the title GREAT BOOKS AND SMALL GROUPS.

FOREWORD

Dr. Davis' initial survey report described the characteristics of people in Great Books groups and the effects they reported from that experience. His second, published in this volume, by analyzing in the same terms those who dropped out as well as those who remained in groups, added considerably to the statistical reliability of the first, showing, for example, that the *apparent* increase in knowledge of literary figures and events was also a *real* increase, not an artifact due to the dropping out of those who showed less gain.

This supplemental report deals with a new and important question through the study of drop-outs and retention (a) among individuals of varying characteristics, and particularly (b) in groups with varying *proportions* of members showing these characteristics. In Dr. Davis' words, "Essentially this report consists of a series of studies, all oriented around the problem of locating and understanding the factors which keep people in Great Books and those which lead them to drop out of the program." These *factors in program retention* are distinguished into two orders: "individual-level factors," which by themselves tend to make individuals want to stay in the group; and "group-level factors," arising out of the *composition of the group as a totality*. Thus, for example, an *individual* who is consistently active in the discussion is statistically more likely to stay, one who is inactive to drop out; but in a *group* with a high proportion of active members, *even the inactive tend to stay*. In such a case, the group's composition has proved more effective than the individual tendencies among its separate members.

The study is therefore important in two ways. For adult educators, it points to a new and effective method for assessing the *holding* properties of groups within their programs. Since, as the earlier reports pointed out, the *effects* of the program showed consistent gains the longer a person stayed in it, it is apparent that any educational program intended to bring about change in its participants must know how to *identify the factors which tend to hold people* in it.

On the other side of this coin, however, the study is merely making use of an adult education setting as the basis for a broad attack on *group-compositional factors,* an area of increasing study in many fields of sociological inquiry: for example, the effects of homogeneity and heterogeneity in suburban developments, or mixed groups of school children; of racial or religious or political proportionality in social or work groups; and many others. The general question is, "Given people who possess some particular characteristic, will they behave differently in groups which vary in the proportion having that characteristic?"

Part I of the study, which I have very briefly summarized here, explains the methodological problem and the mode of attack on it; and reports the results of the investigation of "Group Factors in Program Retention," including considerations of leadership and discussion techniques. This part was written by Dr. Davis, Carolyn Huson, and Joe Spaeth. Part II is a separate consideration of the interconnections among a variety of *individual* factors, and is omitted here as adding less than Part I does to the findings already summarized in the Report to which this digest is appended. The whole of this third report will become available through other channels; the present digest is intended only to call attention to the *group dimension* in the total Great Books program experience.

John Walker Powell

CHAPTER I

Group Composition as a Factor in Program Retention

In terms of sociological inquiry, the data from our survey could be looked at as either 1,909 individuals who happen to be in 172 discussion groups, or as 172 discussion groups which happen to contain 1,909 individuals. This led us to wonder how much of the retention process could be allocated to *individual* factors (the characteristics of people as individuals which affect their continuation) and how much to *group* factors (the characteristics of groups as groups which affect the retention of their members).

Given people who possess some particular characteristic, will they behave differently in groups which vary in the proportion (of members) having that characteristic?

The characteristics selected as variables, to be studied in relation to each other, are of five kinds:

1. Factors in the discussion process:
    Length of exposure
    Size of group
    Member contacts outside of group meetings
    Activity in discussion
    Perceived relevance of program to local issues
    Gain in ability to accept previously rejected schools of thought
    Perceived impact of the program

2. Social structural characteristics:
    Marital status
    Age
    Sex
    Socio-economic status

3. Intellectual characteristics:
    Knowledge of books and literary events (picture test)
    Level of reading quality
    Educational attainment

4. Ideological positions:
    Political preference
    Religious preference

5. Outside interaction:
    Community affairs
    Community involvement
    Visiting

It is evident that there is more than one *kind* of factor involved. Some, like sex, age, or education, are characteristics the individual simply brings to the group. Some, like test scores and gains in insight or acceptance, may be thought of as among the *effects* of the program on the members. Others, like extra-group contacts or reading level, might be either. Length of exposure to the program is, by itself, merely a calendar factor; but it has some initial correlation with many others, since the previous study indicated that *all effects increased steadily with length of exposure* to the program.

1. *Attendance*

Looking first at the over-all attendance, the data show that 64% of the enrollees continued during the year, and 36% dropped out of their groups. Of the 163 groups in the follow-up study, 37% lost up to half their members and 28% lost less than a third. (There were also gains during the period by the accrual of new members after the date of the original survey.)

2. *Discussion Characteristics*

Data on losses by *age of the group* (how many years it had run) show a shakedown effect, with first-year groups losing from half to two-thirds of their members, while groups after two to four or more years lost only about 30% to 50%. Contrary to most sociological and educational expectations, *size* of the group appeared to have no effect on drop-out: groups of ten or less lost 49%, groups of eleven to twenty lost about the same; those with twenty-one to twenty-four members lost, over-all, 38%; and groups of twenty-five or more 45%.

The proportion of new and old members seemed to have little effect, though over-all drop-out rates are somewhat lower when the proportion of new members is about half. The loss rate in all groups is highest for new members. Presumably, the people who don't find Great Books to their liking discover this during the first year.

The next five variables — member contacts outside the group, seeing program relevance to local issues, ability to change views, activity in the discussion, and the feeling that the program is having "a real impact" on the respondent — appear to have definite influence on over-all retention. While *individuals* showing these effects tend to stay longer than those who do not show them, it is also true that *the higher the proportion of those showing the effect,* the higher the retention *even of those who do not.* It is probable that the individuals showing these effects contribute to a climate favorable to keeping *other* people interested: that they "radiate" the effects on them to others in the group.

The possible causal relations among these factors are discussed, and the suggestion is made that outside *contacts* lead to *activity* in discussion which finds *relevance to issues* of concern, thereby creating a climate in which *other views* are acceptable, and so giving the individual a sense of the *impact* of the program.

Selecting three characteristics as basic: contacts, activity, and change, the data show retention highest where the *first two* are high, and lowest where the *second two* are low. In general, high activity led to higher retention, no matter how the other two varied. The same was true of groups showing a high rate of change of views, even when activity was less. Outside contacts, however, proved ambiguous: among groups which are low on both activity and change, high outside contacts is an unfavorable sign, while in combination with either of the others it acts favorably. In terms of an *individual's* behavior, regardless of his own activeness or contacts or willingness to change, his *probability of dropping out tends to vary with the composition of his group.*

In summary:

1) High levels of group activity lead to high retention, independently of the group variables of outside contact and change, and also independently of the individual characteristics involved.
2) High levels of intellectual change lead to high retention.
3) High levels of outside contacts lead to high retention rates only if they also lead to high activity and change. If not, high levels of outside contact are an unfavorable characteristic. This group effect occurs independently of the effect of individual characteristics.

Or, in other words, high levels of sociability are a bad sign unless connected with the *serious* concerns of the program.

3. *Social Structural Characteristics*

Neither marital status nor age composition showed conclusive effects on the holding power of the group. Although Great Books holds more of its married members and more of its older members, the composition of the group in terms of age and marital status doesn't increase or decrease its holding power. Retention tends to rise with the proportion of male members, heavily female groups showing high loss rates; but men are much more likely to be named as active participants, and in groups with similar rates of actives, sex composition makes no difference. The effect of sex composition on retention is apparently solely through its effect on the group's activity level. Groups of high-activity women also showed high retention; but in all groups where more than half were actives, those with more men showed the higher retention.

Socio-economic status, determined somewhat arbitrarily along an axis that puts self-employed professionals and major executives at the top, shows a group effect, *fewer* people of both higher and lower status levels dropping out when the *proportion of high-status* members was large. This again is somewhat dependent on discussion factors (contacts, activity, change), since drop-outs were high when these were low even though the group *had* a majority of high-status members; but high-status members, who tend also to be high in education and outside activity, are likely to be active in discussion.

4. *Intellectual Characteristics*

Of these three — picture-test score, education, and reading levels — one seems to be partly an effect of program exposure; one, a factor not modified by program exposure; and one is ambiguous. Picture-test scores, while not perfectly correlated, do seem to show a "radiating effect" favorable to group retention, low-scorers generally dropping out more frequently but *staying* in groups with a high proportion of high-scorers.

Reading levels were dichotomized into "highbrow" (Camus, Proust, Strindberg) and "middlebrow" (Cozzens, Peter Marshall). As the *proportion of middlebrows* increased, middlebrows dropped out *at a higher rate* than highbrows, who showed higher retention throughout. Looking at it the other way, middlebrows dropped out *less* often if the group showed a higher proportion of highbrows. This factor showed no relationship with the discussion factors.

Educational attainment, usually the research worker's best friend, shows a marked peculiarity at one point in the correlations. It does show a group-compositional effect, both graduates and nongraduates having lower drop-out rates when the proportion of graduates is either below 35% or above 55%. But when the graduates are between 40% and 49% of the group, *both* populations show a sharp peak in drop-out rate. There is a curious implication in the relation between education and outside contacts, however: high proportions of graduates with high degrees of contact are favorable for retention; low proportions of graduates with high degrees of contact, unfavorable. The suggestion is that college people maintain intellectual interests in their outside contacts, while for the less educated person and group, it may be that the intellectual discussions in the program *differ* considerably from their outside patterns of talk and association. If so, patterns developed in the outside arena might tend to inhibit free and easy group discussion of intellectual affairs. However, the likelier solution is that groups which are *homogeneous* on education have higher rates of outside contacts, since friends tend to be homogeneous on most social characteristics, and we do notice that the highest percentages of outside contacts are in our extreme (most-educated, least-educated) groups. The danger zone of college-graduate *proportion* is in the fearsome forties, namely 40% to 49%: over-all drop-outs are highest in groups with this proportion, though for no reason we can assign.

Education and social status show a high correlation, as usual. When they are correlated with drop-out, higher retention is shown by the high-status groups and by the college graduates (with the aforementioned exception of groups with forty to forty-nine per cent of the latter).

On the whole, the net effect of intellectual characteristics is clearly favorable to *individual* retention. But, in terms of effects upon the *group*, high test scores generally are a favorable sign in terms of composition; high proportions of highbrows are helpful in holding the non-highbrows; and only in the higher ranges is education a uniformly beneficent group characteristic, educational *heterogeneity* appearing to be an *un*favorable omen.

5. *Ideological Positions*

The two factors of religious and political preference were selected because in them ideological and value considerations are at the forefront, individuals differing in them will differ in their opinions on many of the readings, and the results of the inter-correlations will shed some light on the diversity of values in group discussion. Politically, the total sample consisted of 48% Democrats, 41% Republicans, and 10% independents; but to simplify the analysis, the members of the groups are dichotomized simply into Democrats and non-Democrats, so that the *proportion Democratic* can be studied as a group-level variable.

There is no difference of moment between the rates at which Democrats and non-Democrats drop out; nor does the total drop-out rate vary continuously with the proportion Democratic. But there are two things of interest in the proportional chart: when that proportion is too low or too high, total drop-out rates are highest; they are lowest when the Democratic proportion is between 50% and 59%. This suggests that a nearly balanced diversity — with a slight majority of Democrats — tends to lead, partly through the resultant discussion activity, to increased retention.

In the matter of religion, there is again a tendency for totally homogeneous groups (all Protestant or all Jewish, the only cases presented) to show higher than average drop-out. Various tables are included in the Report showing differential drop-out rates among members of each religion in the presence of one or more of the others. Since Protestants were present in the largest number of groups, an additional computation was made for Protestantism as a factor affecting the group's holding power. The finding is that non-Protestants tend generally to show higher retention as the proportion of Protestants increases; but as the proportion approaches 100%, Protestants themselves begin to drop out at a greater rate than others. Testing for inter-correlation with other retention-favoring variables leads to the conclusion that diversity is probably a good thing.

6. *Outside Interaction*

By this is meant interest, and involvement, in community or other affairs outside the group; and social visiting other than group contacts outside the meeting. Dividing those with predominantly local interests from non-locals, the data show that *the greater the proportion of members who have high interest,* the better the group does in holding its members — including the non-locals. However, the data also suggest strongly that this is true chiefly because high interest leads to high levels of discussion activity, which had already proved to be a major factor in retention. This is also shown to hold in the case of people actively *involved* in the activities of numbers of organizations, local or national. As to *sociability,* groups show *rising* drop-outs when the proportion of people who spend five or more evenings a month in informal visiting rises to more than half of the group. Groups markedly *low* in sociable members also show some increase in drops, the optimum appearing to be around fifty-fifty. *High status* appears to operate in a way *parallel* to organizational activity, but *independently* of it; and the same could be true with sociability. In short, groups that hold their members tend to include either high-interest people active in affairs, or high-status people, or both. Roughly speaking, it appears that high levels of *serious* outside interaction are a good sign, but, beyond a certain point, high levels of sheer sociability are a bad sign. Groups whose members have a limited range of social interaction do poorly, but so do groups with high amounts of non-serious social interaction. It is groups of people characterized by high rates of participation in serious affairs that seem to do particularly well.

7. *Summary*

Fifteen of our eighteen selected characteristics show some effect on the holding power of a group; particularly when they occur in certain understandable relations with each other. It would appear that, in the Great Books program, the group is somewhat more than a vehicle providing an opportunity for self-expression. The climates created by various compositions seem to play an important part in the success of the program — at least as measured by maintenance of membership.

The *group* factors are not merely an extension of the individual factors. Six of the group variables may operate through "radiating" individual effects as influences moving others in the same direction; but eight other group factors do not. Hence, the group process is not merely one of accentuating individual-level effects.

Group level variables affecting retention, then, are: activity (probably the most important), outside contacts with group members, gains in knowledge and in intellectual breadth, perceived impact from the program; education, local interest and involvement, moderate sociability; proportion of Protestants, Democrats, and people of high status; and the proportion of males. Age, exposure, marriage, reading level, are individually favorable when higher than the median. Religion appears less important. Heterogeneity is useful in some characteristics (politics), homogeneity probably in others (education).

Leadership and Discussion Techniques

The suggestion implicit in the data thus far, that certain combinations of characteristics in certain proportions within a group tend to hold the members together, seems to leave aside the factors of leadership method and discussion techniques, ordinarily assumed to be of major importance in program effectiveness and member retention. Therefore, the data were further studied to see whether leadership method and discussion techniques had a demonstrable relationship to program retention.

1. *Leadership:* Three methods have been used in Great Books: (a) co-leadership by two people; (b) single leader; (c) rotation of leadership among the group members. In addition, while a consistent attempt has been made to give all leaders some prior training, both in the content and in the techniques of discussion, the rapid spread of groups led inevitably to numbers of untrained leaders being pressed into service, in any of the three forms of leader organization.

Since there are no data on the actual quality of leadership, correlations were sought among forms of leadership, training of leaders, and drop-out. The rate of drop-out remained between 27% and 37% whether both leaders had had training, or only one, or none, or the leadership merely rotated. A slight apparent advantage in groups having one trained and one untrained leader vanished when the "activity" factor was introduced: training or the lack of it showed only a six-percentage-point differential in drop-outs from high-activity groups (20% to 26%), and a spread of only three percentage points in low-activity group losses (41% to 44%). Within this very slight spread, however, drop-outs were consistently *less* with untrained than with trained leaders. Remember, however, that "trained" here means only having had a few training sessions in Great Books; it does *not* of necessity mean the lack of already high leadership skill and experience.

2. *Styles of Discussion:* The Great Books Foundation, both in its training courses and in its Leaders' Guides, has certain strongly expressed preferences or rules for leadership. The leader, for example, is to keep the discussion on the book; is to function only by asking questions; is not to express his own opinions at any time; is not to introduce the discussion, and not to summarize it; is not to give any historical or biographical background; should keep participation spread evenly, by discouraging the talkative and, if necessary, calling on less talkative members by name; and should focus on clarification, both of what the author said and of what the group members are trying to say about it.

Asked for their opinion of five leadership roles, three of which agree with the Foundation and two of which were stated in a way contrary to its recommendation, slightly more than half the respondents agree with the Foundation on opinion-giving, background-supplying, and restraining the over-talkative; slightly less than half agree on summarizing or on "cross-examining" participants for purposes of clarification. Some group-composition effects are suggested by the facts that more people who want summaries drop out than non-summarizers, but the more "summarizers" there are in a group, the higher the drop-out rate for *both;* and that the drop-out rate is highest in the groups where most people want to hear the leader's own opinions.

Taking the desire to have the leader summarize the discussion as an independent variable, cross-correlations show that groups with a high proportion wanting the leader to summarize tend to be *lower* on activity and on willingness to change views: i.e., it is suggested, perhaps more dependent or "lazy."

A closer look at groups in which the *leader's* and the *members'* views on these matters of technique are *in opposition* shows that drop-outs are highest where *the group is for* some technique that *the leader is against* — whether the technique is one approved by the Foundation or not.

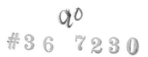